More to Mealtimes

How to help your child
learn almost everything in the kitchen
and make mealtimes easier!

By Kathryn Lord

Award-Winning Author,

Nanny and Professional Organiser

Foreword by Action Amanda

Mabel & Stanley Publishing

Dedication

As with all my books, I am dedicating this book to you, the reader.

I am writing this book because I have listened to all the problems parents have felt in all routines but particularly feeding children, getting them to eat, struggling to think of what to make day in and day out… I get it.

I have worked in households as an after-school Nanny or full-time nanny for over a decade now, having different dynamics, different ages, a different number of siblings and knowing their likes and dislikes, all the while creating a balanced, healthy, and interesting meal plan, as well as supporting children to learn along the way. So, to you, I hope this book will make your life easier.

But I am also dedicating this book to all the children it could impact in a positive way. I truly believe supporting children with basic life skills such as cooking and all that goes with it, will help them become successful in all areas for their future.

Love Kat

Contents

Foreword

When I first met Kat, I was inspired by her dedication to improving children's lives and I was privileged when she asked me to write the foreword for this amazing book.

As a children's champion myself and having spent the last 30 years committed to helping children lead active, healthy lives, Kat's approach to childcare and child development really resonated with me.

Kat has exceptional organisation skills; she's dedicated, knowledgeable and is not afraid to think outside of the box. I know that this book will be an invaluable addition to her 'More to' series and a must-have for parents and carers seeking an organised and creative way to ensure that their children develop, and enjoy, healthy eating habits that will last a lifetime.

Amanda Frolich aka Action Amanda, The Children's Champion

Chapter 1
Introduction

As with organising, mealtimes are something that I have been thinking about for a long time. Both of my 'More to' books and my More to Organising workshops heavily involve food. I was asked to create a workshop for one nursery as their OFSTED inspection recommended supporting their children to eat more healthily, and so I started to incorporate healthy eating in all of them. There is so much development to be enabled through food but more than that, I have supported families for over 9 years to create balanced diets (not dieting) for children from babies to teens.

Through my business- More to Organising, I have supported many families to organise their kitchens. Often clients will say that I won't find any out-of-date foods. Guess how many clients didn't have 'gone- off' foods? None.

I used to be the third checker at Marks and Spencer's food when I was at university. This was the late shift after a full day of lectures and after two other people had already checked the dates. I would still find products that had passed their sell by date. While dates are something more of a guideline, and I am not saying you shouldn't use those foods- generally; with herbs and spices, they will just not be as flavourful for example - but other items like garlic can cause serious illness, (botulism if you're wondering). If you are a parent, it is totally at your discretion to feed the out-of-date items to your children, but just be wary that children's stomachs are not as strong as adult ones so can be affected more easily. If you are a Nanny and that child gets sick, you might be liable.

In my second book, I help families organise their spaces to support their tricky day- to day routines so if the sleep routines are tricky, organise their bedroom. If the school run is hard to get going, organise your hallway and uniforms; similarly. organising your kitchen can really help with mealtimes.

I have spoken to so many Mums about how difficult they find mealtimes. How they never know what to cook, that the children won't eat what they make, that snacks are taking over the day. I feel very strongly about helping children to have a healthy relationship with food.

When I was a teacher, I had a little girl who was anorexic and a little boy who was bulimic. They were both 7. While these are extreme cases and were a result of deeper mental health issues, I became more mindful of how I reacted to food around them, I thought more about the language I used and learnt more about how to support children with this.

Personally, I come from a generation where we got what was put on the table and we couldn't get down from the table until we ate everything. I also grew up associating food with comfort. I can tell you; I had an awful relationship with food. I put myself on a diet when I was 14; I have "yoyo" dieted with everything from Slimming World, Weight Watchers, Juice Plus and Aloe Forever until I started marathon running and learnt that food is fuel. I learnt why I need my proteins and carbohydrates, I found out which nutrients were great for recovery. That is not to say I don't enjoy food, I really do (carb loading is my favourite) but my relationship with food is so much healthier. I no longer stepped on the scales a few times a day and other things got healthier like my skin, hair, and nails as a result. I learnt about balance and not restricting, and this is what I want for our next generation. For my continuing professional development, I studied weaning and child nutrition. I also follow lots of child nutritionists on social media to keep my knowledge up to date. It is all very well me knowing all this, but I really feel we should educate our children with this information.

This book will go through the importance of empowering our children with the knowledge of what we should eat, how and why we need gut diversity, how to get children involved in all parts of the process, help you to create your own meal plans which in turn helps you to batch cook and thinking for their future, how to be sustainable in sourcing, storing, utilising and not wasting food which helps the planet but also helps save money and time.

But the secret sauce in all I do is how to do this while supporting child development in a fun and purposeful way.

Chapter 2

Nutrition

'Kids Eat in Colour' is a great account on social media that empowers parents to educate our children. Rather than saying food is good or bad, there is guidance on how to use the correct age and appropriate language to explain what different 'colours' help with.

I have just had my bloods taken, just for a health check. You will be happy to know that I am ok on everything but one thing; I am low in HDL or Good Cholesterol. This means I need to eat more avocado and salmon, so said the nurse. I love both of those so that won't be a problem, other than they can be more costly than other foods. I must admit, I buy my avocados frozen, and it is all about getting into the habit of defrosting them if I want to eat them not in a smoothie. Head to the chapter on Meal Ideas for a recipe for what we called "poo juice" or just chocolate milkshake to the girls I looked after. Adding frozen avocado into a smoothie is a great way to get it into their tummies if your children say they don't like it.

Anyway, while looking up other foods that could enhance my good cholesterol, other than nuts as they give me a rash, I discovered purple fruits and vegetables. When I encourage children to eat the rainbow throughout the week for gut diversity, purple and blue fruits and vegetables are the ones we have to research the most. The obvious ones are aubergine, blueberries and purple grapes but often forgotten are blackberries. Apparently black raspberries are also a thing and red cabbage can also help. My favourite ingredient that I can add into my diet is dark chocolate (with at least 75% cocoa content) and if you'd like a recipe for that, head to Summer Snacks, in Chapter Seven.

So, in light of the purple vegetables, I encourage my children to eat the rainbow and not skittles. Getting them involved is really important so while I am going to talk about this now in more detail, I highly recommend that you draw a rainbow and research the different colour fruits and vegetables. If they have not tried a fruit or vegetable, add it to your Try- it Tuesday menu plan (More on that in Meal Planning in Chapter 5). Here are some of the ones we found. If it has seeds then it is a fruit, so the argument that pineapples are not allowed on pizzas falls flat if the reason is that it is a fruit, because so are tomatoes. Just saying!

When I went to a Children's nutrition course, the course provider said that trying to eat at least one green vegetable everyday has the most benefits. If you do find ones that we haven't, please let us know on Instagram tagging @more_to_organising:

Red – red onions, radishes, red cabbage (is it red or purple?), tomatoes, red peppers, Strawberries, red apples, raspberries, watermelon, cherries

Orange – carrot, sweet potato, orange, orange peppers, butternut squash, pumpkin

Yellow – corn, baby corn, corn on the cob, onions, parsnip, yellow peppers, bananas, pineapples

Green – cabbage, broccoli, edamame beans, peas, spinach, lettuce, leeks, chives, asparagus, string beans, avocado pear, green peppers, cucumber, green apples, kiwi, lime, pears, grapes, melons

Blue and purple – aubergine, blueberries, beetroot, red cabbage (is it red or purple?), grapes, blackberries, blackcurrants, black raspberries

I met The Rainbow Fairy when we both spoke at NannyPalooza. Natasha Gavin ran a workshop, 'I know why it's yum Mum,' sharing her message about nutrition to nurseries and parents. I loved what she did and hired her for my own nanny children. She had these amazing Top Trump cards which I still use to this day when I work as a nanny, tutor or even just with friends. They have fascinating information about the energy, strength, protection, digestion and brain power our foods give us. So, I will let you in on these amazing nuggets of information while talking about all the things we need to add into our meals.

Carbohydrates

For some reason, carbohydrates got really bad press when I was growing up. And in most of my yo-yo dieting experiences, it was banned. As I mentioned, I learnt a lot about fuelling my body when I started training properly for marathons and understanding that our bodies need carbohydrates. It is a source of energy and helps to control our blood glucose and insulin. Carb-loading the day before a marathon, (I start a few days before and continue long after) is a strategy to build up glycogen in the muscles so you can run for longer. The problem with carbohydrates is not the humble potato or the trusty rice, but all those carbohydrates that are processed with other less nutritious ingredients. Think white bread, cake, and biscuits. I am sure you already know what I am going to say about those. There is a time and a place for bread, cake, and biscuits, it is about balance, and I will suggest you serve them, just not for every meal. The most ridiculous thing about the diets from my generation was that being told to cut out carbohydrates is actually impossible. Many fruits and vegetables also contain carbohydrates.

Oats

Let's start at the start of the day here. Overnight oats or porridge are spoken about more in the section on breakfast. If you can start the day with oats, the Rainbow Fairy says they are full of fibre, iron, and minerals that are released slowly into our bodies.

Wheat

If we are going to eat bread, wholemeal is better for us as it is less processed. It is a great source of fibre which we need to keep our bowels moving and is a source of energy.

Potatoes

Why do all children like chips? I didn't! Someone came into our school when I was about 10 and told us how awful chips were for us and as a susceptible child, I listened. Did you know all potatoes are poisonous to us if they are raw? That's just a fun fact for you. I can't really remember much of what was said but I then refused to eat them. I can understand my Mum's frustration now after feeding many children who turn around and say they no longer want to eat a food that they had eaten many times before, however, my defiant act meant I ended up actually disliking chips for real. Back then, chips were deep fried and eating a cold chip left a layer of fat at the top of my mouth that I just can't describe. It took me many years before I started eating chips again. Even at University, I would buy cheesy chips and give the non- cheesy chips to people in the taxi queue, just so I could move up the queue and get home faster. It worked, and no, we didn't have Uber back then! I have started to eat chips in my thirties again, but only because they are not deep fried. And I quite like sweet potato fries too.

Many children don't actually know that chips are made from potatoes! I think there is a time and a place for processed foods but making your own is so much better for your bodies. So let us not chastise the chip, it's just a long thin roast potato, but let us think about balance. The great thing about being able to make your own chips is that you can use cutters to make them wavy or straight. You can move to a knife when developmentally appropriate. At first, after your child has peeled the potato, I would cut it in half so it doesn't wobble when they try to cut the lengths but when they are ready, they can learn to hold the potato safely and do it for themselves. Not only is that a good skill to have, but a bag of potatoes is much cheaper and much more versatile than a bag of chips. According to The Rainbow Fairy, Natasha Gavin, potatoes give us Vitamin C and B AND we can eat the rainbow through potatoes because their skins can be white, purple, red or blue!

Pasta

Just like having a chicken breast is not a whole meal, neither is only having pasta.

I worked as a nanny in Italy for a few summers and fell in love with Chingiale Pappardelle, that's wild boar by the way. The children loved it too. Many names for pasta are translated into English as insects or minibeasts: Vermicelli means little worms and Farfalle means butterflies. The children I currently look after come to my house in the holidays for a special trip to the playground near to my house, and during the summer we have picnics. They think it is hilarious as one time a dog came and ate my sandwich, and they talk about it often, but when it is too cold to do that, in October Half Term and February Half Term, we have pasta at my house. My pasta in Italian is called tricolore pasta on account of the fact that it comes in three colours. The green pasta is made with spinach and the red is made with tomato, while the yellow is just normal pasta. We have that with bolognaise or pasta sauce and then add lots of vegetables too!

There are other carbohydrate options such as couscous, rice, quinoa, and noodles.

Red fruits and vegetables

Peppers can come in red, yellow, green and orange but I am going to pop it here, and only talk about them once! Peppers are a source of Vitamin A which helps our bodies against catching colds. The Rainbow Fairy also says, just like carrots, they can help us to see in the dark. Strawberries contain lots of vitamin C which helps us absorb iron. We need iron because it helps our brain and blood. Raspberries are similar to strawberries in benefits. Baked beans are a source of protein so great for your meat free Monday meals.

Tomatoes are an antioxidant, with vitamins A and C to keep us healthy.

Orange Fruit and Vegetables

Everyone knows that carrots help us see in the dark, but did you know that they also help our skin? Sweet potatoes also have lots of vitamins as well as potassium and iron. That means they boost our immune system and also give us lots of energy.

Yellow Fruits and Vegetables

Sweetcorn has vitamin A, B and C but is also a source of carbohydrate, as it is high in fibre, and therefore it helps digestion. Citrus fruits can be orange or yellow and are great for vitamin C. The Rainbow Fairy says that Vitamin C helps get rid of "harmful waste products" from our body.

Green Fruits and Vegetables

Broccoli contains minerals such as iron and calcium as well as vitamins, and these help almost everything in our body including our bones.

Apples have two types of fibre- insoluble and soluble. One helps our digestive system and the other helps our heart. Peas are actually more nutritious when you eat them frozen or cold as boiling them gets rid of good nutrients. Rocket is in the same family as broccoli and cabbage so it's worth adding some to your plate. Spinach has lots of vitamins and minerals- heat it in a pan with lemon and it is so delicious. The darker green the vegetable is, the better it is for us. Cabbage is a dark green veg packed with vitamins and fibre. Kale is as good as broccoli; in one Nanny family, the girls loved home-made kale chips. Brussel sprouts help our skin as well as our digestive system.

Purple or blue fruit and vegetables

Plums are great for helping you poo as they are high in fibre and help your immune system as it is packed full of vitamin A. Blackberries are full of vitamin C which according to The Rainbow Fairy helps your body to make collagen, which keeps our skin firm. Grapes help us to rehydrate. Dried raisins and prunes give iron which is good for our blood and give us lots of energy, just make sure you brush your teeth well after.

White vegetables

Onions and garlic are alliums which also include chives and leeks. These are amazing for fighting germs. The Rainbow Fairy says they are "antifungal, antiviral and antibacterial".

Seeds

Pumpkin seeds are brilliant because they are packed with zinc, and sunflower seeds are full of vitamin E. They both have Omega oils which keep our heart healthy and our brains thinking.

This book is not about weaning. It is really important to seek the correct information when transitioning from purees to solids. Follow the guidelines on not adding salts or sugars into babies' foods. While I do talk about hazards in the health and well-being section, this book is for toddlers and above as you will see in the prepping section, there are developmentally appropriate tasks that they can start with and move along as they get more confident.

Action

***make a fruit and vegetable rainbow with your children!**

Post it on Instagram tagging @more_to_organising with the hashtags #moretomealtimes #fruitandvegrainbow

Chapter 3

Child Involvement

I was watching Teletubbies when I was far too old to be watching a toddler show, but in the middle, where you watch something in the tummy of the Teletubby, a boy and his father were making Egg Mayonnaise. I can't actually remember how old I was, and at least one of my parents was in the house, but I put it upon myself to make my own egg mayonnaise. Thankfully, it all went very smoothly, and I also cleared up the evidence too. There were also times that my friend and I would make crazy smoothies (that included ice cream and biscuits), cheese toasties and the least nutritional value "snack" of butter and sugar mixed together. I think the thing that we were great at was making sure my parents never knew we had made such snacks. I don't think children should be making foods that involve sharp knives, boiling water, and dangerous equipment without adult supervision. However, I strongly believe that the more we involve the children in all the parts of the process, the more they will develop the skills to be able to use said knives and equipment safely, which reduces unnecessary accidents and gets them into the habits of prepping and clearing up, which will help in their futures.

While I am going to talk about this more in the related chapters, I will talk now about techniques that I have used to get the children involved. If you want children to eat the food that is on their plates, then getting them involved is the first step. It is absolutely ok not to like some foods and we should not force children to 'like' anything. It could be a sensory issue. I cannot stand mushrooms. I think it is the slimy texture and they remind me of snails. Before you ask, yes, I have also tried snails at "French day" in Year 6. I know it's not the taste that I dislike because I quite like Truffle oil, as I found out at the Festival du Tortufo in Alba when I worked as a nanny on a Vineyard in Piedmont in my early twenties. What foods do you dislike? Would you like it if you were forced to eat it? If someone made a huge deal of it? It is not to say you never provide that food again, they say it takes up to 18 'exposures' and our tastes change as we get older. Saying that, a phrase I picked up from another nanny was, 'don't yuk my yum,' which basically means, let's agree to disagree that I like it and you don't. I think this is so important when you have siblings that can influence each other to not try foods that they might like. I am always wary of how children react in front of their younger siblings if they don't like a particular food. Creating a positive environment when trying new foods is important, it is not to say that older siblings have to eat foods they don't like, but having an agreed way to dispose of foods that they are re-trying, such as using a tissue and disposing of it, rather than spitting it out and creating an ordeal, is a much more positive strategy. It is actually much easier to do this when you start younger with children. As a nanny, sometimes children have not got into the habit of trying new foods, textures or flavours before I started working with them, whereas if you plan it into your routine, such as 'try it Tuesdays' - as we will talk about in chapter five on Meal Planning, where you add a new food to a plate of things you know they already love and eat – it will become much more the 'norm.'.

Planning

I was working with a 9-year-old whose preferences changed over the years I was her nanny and, while I do think there were outside influences such as her friends' preferences, I also think having autonomy over her food choices made her feel more confident. You would not like it if you were told what you will eat. You would not like it if you had no choices. To empower her to make mealtimes a happier time for everyone, including her siblings (but also me!) I focussed on the foods she does enjoy, while also discussing variation in her food intake. We talked about the different types of proteins and carbohydrates she does love, and then we created a kind of jigsaw, so she didn't have the same food types next to each other. We also considered the school menu to create diversity within the day. I am happy to tell you that fruit and vegetable intake have never been a problem with the children in this family, but making sure your children don't only eat carrots every day is important; don't forget to eat the rainbow, if not daily, then definitely over the week. Making a drawing of a rainbow and researching all the different fruits and vegetables is something that I have done with several families and taught in workshops for Nannies and Parents.

While we will talk about reading and writing opportunities again in the next chapter, getting into the habit of this seasonally helps them into adulthood. Pouring through recipe books every quarter helps to keep your meal planning interesting but also means as their food preferences change, you can update or expand what is on the menu. Even with all this knowledge and these habits, I still sometimes get into a rut. But I also love having different foods in different seasons; I would never have a Roast in Summer; I don't really have salads in Winter. I prefer Sushi in Summer and I prefer Soup in Winter. Because of the supermarkets, we now have all fruits and vegetables available all year round, but, if we learn to eat them when they are at their best, they taste better; it is also better for the planet (more on that in Chapter 9 - Sustainability).

Sourcing

In my career, I have worked with some of the most disadvantaged children during my time as a teacher across Manchester, and the most advantaged children as a nanny. Whether children eat processed foods, or whether they have their own chef, they may still not fully understand where their food comes from. When I was a teacher, if you asked the children what they did during the holidays, they would say that they went to the 'big Asda', whereas many of the wealthy nanny children had never been to a supermarket at all. As a teacher and a nanny, I organised trips to go to a farm. The joy that children show when they see lambs or chicks is the same. Yes, children learn that the food on their plate was alive. I am personally not a vegetarian or vegan, but I do try to have meat-free meals or even meat-free days. My mum lives on a small- holding where she has hens, ponies, sheep, goats, cats and dogs, and the children in the nurseries that she owns get to visit often. For two Easters, my mum and I have cared for orphaned lambs, bottle feeding them and getting to have lamb snuggles. We also hatched eggs into chicks who I named Uno and Piccolo. I had already hatched many eggs as a teacher, getting an incubator at the school I worked in and letting every class visit our chicks during lunchtimes. On the farm just up from my mum's barn (yes, she did up a barn to live in), lives a little boy. He sees everything from birth to death and everything in between. Death is sadly a part of life; I think what we need to support our children with, is thinking of the quality of life the animals have and sourcing eggs that are free range for example or reducing our meat intake and buying it from better places where possible.

Sourcing fruit and vegetables is easier. For many nanny families I have worked with, I have taken them to Garson's Farm in Esher which is under an hour from Southwest London- it is a great day trip. You can dig for carrots, choose your pumpkins, pick your berries, find different vegetables that the children might not have eaten before, cut your sunflowers and choose your courgette flowers - you read that right, it was one of my favourite dishes when I lived in Italy. I was so happy when I found out I could get them in

England too- I did also find them at a Farmers Market in Wimbledon, which meant I didn't need to go all the way to Esher every time. They are so versatile. You can stuff them with ricotta or fry them in a flour and water mixture.

There are plenty of pick your own farms all over the country and I find that when the children have picked the vegetables themselves, they are much more likely to try them. For the vegetables that they might not have tried before, use recipe books to find out how to cook them together. I would encourage you to still use the paper versions rather than googling it. Some websites can be good, however; the skills they learn from using the index and going to the correct page number, reading lists, captions and instructions is so valuable for using non- fiction books in other areas of their life as well as informing their own writing. It is not a problem if you don't have many recipe books. My favourite books to take out from the library are recipe books and if you have read my second book on organising, you will know I like to use the library as a way to make sure I do not keep books I do not use in my home. If there is a recipe you love a lot, encourage your young people to create their own handwritten recipe books (which also is a great purposeful writing opportunity).

Growing your own fruit and vegetables is also a brilliant way to source some of your produce. I have worked for families who had the space to grow fruits and vegetables, but then they also had gardeners.

Even without open space, you can grow cress for your scrambled eggs or herbs in pots or on windowsills. Learning to care for something can be a great stepping stone for a child to be able to look after a pet or even a child of their own eventually. Obviously, they will have to learn what they need to help a plant grow.

Prepping

I think it is important to show our children the different cutting boards and talk about food hygiene on their level. Similar good practice includes always washing your hands before touching food, whether making it or eating it, and how important it is to have a clean surface too. In my workshops, I talk about helping children try something new, use new tools and build resilience, but I also discuss what the difference is between wrapping our children up in cotton wool and providing a safe environment. Of course, there are certain things we need to protect our children from, and preventing unnecessary accidents is a must. Through years of being a teacher and gaining my paediatric first aid certificates every three years, I cannot walk into a room without spotting all the hazards that could cause harm to our children. We must provide opportunities for risk taking, but within reason. So, in this part, I will go through different things our children can do to help prepare a meal, that still provide amazing fine motor opportunities but that are differentiated based on their abilities. I am not going to say age- related abilities, as that is the wrong term. These are developmentally- related abilities, you know your child, but make sure you're not holding them back by assuming that they can't do something. Or indeed, they might not be able to do something until you let them practise. This list is not exhaustive. I will talk about other activities you can do to support these skills through play in the next chapter, Child development.

Start with these:

Pouring cold liquids

Counting/sharing pre-cut foods

Pouring peas/sweetcorn

Mixing with a wooden spoon

When they can do that, try these:

Opening a yogurt

Spooning out peas/sweetcorn

Whisking with a fork

Cutting cucumber with a shape cutter

Cutting cookie dough with a shape cutter

Peeling vegetables with a palm peeler

Cracking an egg

After they are confident with the above, they can move on to these with adult supervision:

Mixing with a whisk

Cutting with a knife

Using an adult peeler

These can be done without supervision:

Measuring liquids in jug

Weighing dried foods on a scale

Then supervise with these skills:

Mixing with a handheld blender

Using a blender

Taking something hot from the microwave

Pouring hot water from a kettle

Draining hot water with a sieve

I would say that whilst they are still children, the tasks that I have said to do with supervision stay supervised, because if something does go wrong - and accidents do sometimes happen - then there is an adult present to help. It might be a case of you saying, 'make sure an adult is in the room when you attempt these,' but you may no longer need to be standing right next to them.

Prepping meat- talk about hygiene in terms of raw meat, saying if meat is not cooked it can make us poorly, so we need to wash our hands before and after touching it, as well as surfaces and utensils that have touched it before it is cooked too. The best way to do this is by just doing it. Children really do learn from what they see you doing, so if they are not in the kitchen when you are cooking, how are they to know?

There are a few favourite things that children I work with love to be involved in, and by far it is when I hold up a string of sausages and they use the scissors to snip them. I generally have a queue of the three siblings in my current club eagerly awaiting their turn; what is great about this is that they don't touch the sausages at all, and we do it over the pan. It is such a different way to cut, I make it easier for the youngest by holding the sausages either side of where she needs to cut, whereas for the oldest ones, I just hold the top sausage. Sometimes they are spinning, sometimes they need to snip a few times before it works, this not only helps them with patience and determination, but also perfects their fine motor skills in a different way. It is fun. As soon as we are over, the scissors go straight into the dishwasher.

Another raw meat-handling situation they love to be involved in is making home-made chicken nuggets. Again, this can be differentiated. I generally set out the plates with breadcrumbs on one, egg on another and cut up chicken pieces on another. I teach them to only use one hand to handle the raw chicken, dipping into the raw egg and then into the breadcrumbs before landing on a spare plate, then they always have a free hand that's not contaminated to touch pan handles, utensils, or the tap, which inevitably they will need. As they get more confident with this process, I also let them be in charge of preparing the eggs, breadcrumbs, and chicken if they want to. I think the main thing about this is I don't make them do anything. I tell them what is on the menu as we are walking home from school (which they will have been involved in but may sometimes need a reminder) and they will either ask to help or I will ask if they want to help.

Watching mincemeat brown, and stirring it, is also interesting for children; for their future, knowing what it should look like when it is cooked is a useful skill. If you teach them to hold the pan handle with one hand and hold the top of the wooden spoon with the other, they will have more control and it will be safer. How I start this, is with me holding the handle and them putting one hand on mine or behind their back, and stirring with the other; this prevents them from accidentally touching the hot pan but also means the pan won't accidentally tip. It is so important that they stir slowly so hot meat doesn't flip out of the pan. By practising stirring in the prep phase, you know if and when they are ready to then stir hot foods sensibly.

Cracking eggs is another skill that all children love to try. The more they have a chance to try, the better they are at not getting shell into the food. I generally crack into a cup and have another cup ready for the shells so that they aren't accidentally glooping egg white all over the surface. If bits of shell do end up in the cup, I just scoop them out using the eggshell as it cuts through easily. Pouring the egg into a bowl means it's easier for the child to scoop the shell out. Apparently, just dropping the egg from about 10 cm high into a bowl will crack the shell allowing the membrane to stay intact so no shell ends up in the wrong place. I personally find that method more fiddly than the way I've been doing it since my Teletubby egg mayonnaise days, but the point is, there isn't just one way to do things and it's ok if your child finds a way that works for them; our responsibility is to show them as many ways as possible and let them figure out what is their preferred method (that doesn't just apply to cooking) in a positive, safe way. Some children don't like the feel of raw meat or raw egg, so you can provide a disposable glove, allowing them to still keep one hand free, but it is so important that they don't cross contaminate; pull the glove so it ends up inside out, dispose of it and wash their hands as normal. They should also be able to understand that they must not touch their face while handling raw meat or egg.

Cooking

Again, this should be developmentally appropriate rather than age appropriate. Pressing the buttons on the microwave is different to putting the correct material in and taking it out sensibly when it is hot. In a couple of families, the microwave has been higher up than usual, which is not overly safe for me at 5'2" (and a half) but it is even more dangerous for children who tend to be smaller than me.

I have an anecdote about a microwave, or rather a child using a microwave. It was my cousin and her eldest son; she asked him to put the milk bottle in the microwave for his baby brother. So, he went away with the bottle and came back…without it! She asked him where the bottle was, and he said, "It is in the microwave". He hadn't turned the microwave on! We must think about giving clear instructions and small achievable steps. Some children can only follow one instruction at a time.

It is important to note that when microwaving breast milk, it can leave heat spots which can burn your baby's mouth, so it is better to boil water in a pan, take it off the heat and rest the bottle in the water to warm.

The children don't cook with me every day, but they love to see inside the pans, they love to see the water bubbling and we get a lot of vocabulary and discussion from it. Being part of this helps them understand how to be careful around a hot oven. It is far better to learn by watching and talking than to not know anything, that's when the accidents occur. It is often through naivety or cluelessness, and this can be avoided. Making sure the pan handles are not overhanging is an obvious one, but I also keep the children a couple of steps back. For the really little ones, I will lift them up, and for the little ones, I place a step for them to be able to see at a safe distance.

We were talking about the boiling water spitting just recently, to which the five-year-old said, "Pans don't spit, people do." So, I showed her the bubbling water firing out the pan. I also said that hot oil can also spit, and it can really hurt. While we are working on prevention here, it is also a time to talk about what to do if that did happen. Running a burn under cold water rather than submerging it in a bowl, because the burn actually heats up the water for example or wrapping a severe burn in cling film to prevent infection. Thank goodness chip pans aren't in every home anymore. They caused a lot of house fires.

I was discussing writing this book with a good friend of mine and she said her brother pulled over hot water on himself which caused life changing burns and I discussed it with another education professional, who showed me her own scars from a similar incident.

If the children haven't been cooking with me, they have what is called 'Independent time'. This happens just before tea and just after tea. I will talk about how to get them to be involved in clearing up further in this chapter, but they know that they need to give me space to finish the kitchen, and that works for us. To get them downstairs to eat most of the time, I will ask, "Who wants to be my rice/pasta/chip tester?" and inevitably, all three will want to test them. This not only gives them some autonomy in how they like their foods cooked, but it gives me a chance to serve up while they are debating how many more seconds the carbohydrate needs.

Serving

I always serve one or two raw vegetables, already prepped for as soon as we arrive home. Then the children help me with the other vegetables. They either spoon them, pour them, use a cutter to create shapes, or a peeler and knife to cut them.

For some reason, the children I currently work for are indifferent about mash. Mash is usually the second potato favourite among children after chippies. With regard to food shapes, I am not suggesting you spend hours of your time creating shapes out of foods (I only do it for birthdays, special occasions, and mash potato, it seems), but actually, since the first time I got creative with my current children's food, they have taken the joy away from me by making their own shapes for themselves, or for each other! I made a mashman or mash person (you know, like a snowman or snowperson) by making a body and a head with an ice cream scoop (or similar) and added peas as buttons, sweetcorn as eyes and broccoli (I was taught an easy way to remember how to spell broccoli- it has one stem so only one 'l' and lots of curls so two 'c's', I love giving this little hack to children) as arms. We will talk about learning about different recipes from different cultures, countries and celebrations in Understanding the World, People and Communities, but I also like to make pictures with their food to make a celebration a little bit more exciting. For example, I made bats out of cucumber slices for a birthday, and I made a leprechaun face complete with hat and rainbow, for St Patrick's day and a skeleton for Halloween, all out of vegetables. In my first nanny role, every Friday they had a playdate so with their starter of cucumber, tomato, and cheese, I made a dragon for Chinese New Year, Easter eggs and bunnies for Easter, and Christmas trees with cucumber as the branches, complete with cubed cheese for presents under the tree and cucumber baubles. I made a Pokemon ball out of tomatoes and olives. I even made mice and Santa hats out of strawberries. Getting the children involved in this does make it a lot of fun, they even suggest different vegetables that might work for different parts of a picture. Like I said, don't do this every day, but when you do, it is good. If you want to see more head to www.moretoorganising.com or follow me on Instagram @more_to_organising.

Clearing up

I premise this with the children as teamwork. When I start a job, I lay out my expectations. When the children have finished their meal, they take their plate to the sink. With the parents I work for in the afternoon, we have a good routine going on. I empty the dishwasher, fill it, and put it on in the evening then they empty it, fill it, and put it on in the morning. This routine serves us. If I have time, I will empty the dishwasher before I do the school run but sometimes, I go straight to the school so can't, which is also why I don't expect the children to put their items in the dishwasher. If they have something left on their plate - which is ok because that means they have listened to their body and their hunger cues and sensations and have learnt to know when they feel full, and do not overeat - they scrape it into the food bin. There is a stool for the little one so she can access the areas of the kitchen she needs to.

After dinner, they have independent time. This is time planned into our routine where they have to do something without me. While they are doing that, I put the dishwasher on, wash up things that can't go in there, wipe down the mats and tablecloth then sweep the floor. The children know that if they help with this process, then we will get more time to play together. One of the fun things we do is they move all the chairs to make 'the floor is lava' game, and they use their gross motor skills, balancing skills, and problem-solving skills to get from the kitchen door to the garden door, avoiding the floor while I sweep up. The reason I like this is because we are using a routine that I must do but we are still engaging, chatting, and giggling. The whole process is interesting and fun, I get to get all the crumbs from under the table and they get to survive the boiling hot lava bubbling from the kitchen floor. Another thing they like to do is use the handheld hoover. There have been times that they have argued over who gets to hoover up!

In terms of developmentally appropriate tasks, using plastic plates and plastic cups until they are confident, before then giving ceramic plates and glasses means there will be less disastrous accidents.

In another family, it was developmentally appropriate that they put their plates and cutlery in the dishwasher after breakfast and tea. The two girls could choose who wiped the table and who swept the floor. In several roles, the children have used handheld hoovers to vacuum under the table.

Kitchen Organisation

One of the best things you can do for your children is to organise with them in mind. It helps them become more independent and makes your life easier. If everything is up too high, they will always need you to do things for them! I have helped many families optimise their kitchens by really getting to know their needs and creating systems that work for them. Here are simple things you can do. Create a drawer low down with their plates, bowls, cups, and utensils. Create a snack area that they can access independently, with options they can have all the time. Giving children autonomy over when they feel hungry and when they can eat supports independence. I personally wouldn't put treats in here because treats are just that. It is our responsibility to help our children to have balance. It is not that they are never allowed treats. It is also our responsibility to support them to identify why they want a snack at that time, is it because they are hungry, or are they bored? Are they actually thirsty? It is definitely our responsibility not to create a connection with food and comfort.

Having dried foods in see- through containers means the children can be involved in helping to write the shopping list as they can easily see what you are running low on.

Making a packed lunch station in the fridge helps to make that process easier.

Moreover, organising and creating systems in your kitchen makes mealtimes better for you too. In fact, organising and creating systems in any room in your home makes your whole life easier. If you'd like to know more, read 'More to Organising- how to help your child become more independent and make your life easier' or hire me for in-person or online packages. Head to www.moretoorganising.com to book in.

Actions

***borrow recipe books from the library**

***go to a pick your own farm- put a photo on Instagram with your picks tagging @more_to_organising with the hashtags #moretomealtimes #pickyourown**

***grow your own cress- post it on Instagram tagging @more_to_organising with the hashtags #moretomealtimes #growyourown**

***let your children start to prep the meal with you (developmentally appropriate tasks)**

***make a mashperson-post it on Instagram tagging @more_to_organising with the hashtags #moretomealtimes #mashperson**

***create an expectation of teamwork- get children to put dishes by the sink or in the dishwasher and support clearing up so they build life skills and you have more time to do other things together**

***organise your kitchen with children in mind and optimise your systems for an easier life**

Chapter 4

Child development

I truly believe that so much can be learnt from cooking. There are the obvious areas like maths and science and some people agree that you can also develop your creativity. But I believe we literally can hit every area of the Early Years Foundation Stage, and while this book is not just for our littlest learners, I have mentioned previously, that the younger we start involving our children in being a part of the process the better; the skills they learn help them to become more independent but can also end up making your life easier.

Some of our activities in this section will be out of the kitchen, pre-requisites, or skills they need can be learnt in their play even before we think about food or pans or ovens.

Role Play

The one thing I think all homes should have is a role play kitchen- it is known that children learn by watching what adults do and how that is reiterated is through role play. We will talk about the role play kitchen in the reading, writing and physical development section within this chapter too, but before pencil touches paper, before spoon touches pan, there is a whole lot of talking, turn taking and fun to be had.

In my second book, I talk about when I first got the nanny job I am still in now (while writing this book- not necessarily while you are reading it, although both could be true) where the then three-year-old would always make me a pretend cup of tea every day because her parents always offered me a real cup of tea. I am happy to report that the parents still do this to this day, but if this is not a perfect example of learning from what they see, I don't know what is.

Mud kitchen - As much as parents might hate that the children come home with messy jumpers or dirty summer dresses, having a child come home completely clean probably means the children haven't explored to their heart's content. There is a lot of sensory development to be had in the mud kitchen. Learning about how the soil feels, ripping up leaves and snapping twigs. The imagination that comes from 'cooking' in a mud kitchen leads to role play with others and thus extends their vocabulary. When I was a little girl, we had a quarter of an acre of garden to play in. One of my favourite things to do was collect leaves, sticks and petals then mix them with the freshly cut grass that my dad left in piles from his lawnmower that looked like a go- cart. I remember making soups and pretending that the different colours of leaves were different ingredients. I remember adding in water from the hose pipe making it look like noodle soups with all the vegetables floating around. Then when I had friends over, we would create a café and make concoctions for each other. Don't worry, we knew not to eat it. I am just saying, before someone invented the mud kitchen, in the mid 90's, we were already learning this way in a self-motivated, exploratory way. I don't know if my parents were aware I ever did that, other than a plastic bowl arriving back in the kitchen worse off than when it left!

Personal, Social, Emotional Development

Social Development - Remember when I said the three-year-old made me a pretend cup of tea because her parents always offered me a real cup of tea? I don't know if it's terribly British, but the social etiquette of offering someone a drink when they come to your house is a habit that children will take through to adulthood with them. More than that, playing in a role play kitchen or mud kitchen, starts the personal skills of taking turns, figuring out social cues, overcoming differences and solving conflicts.

Managing feelings

I still don't know if this is also a uniquely British trait, but tea seems to be the answer to everything. Cold-have a cup of tea, thirsty- have a cup of tea, sad-have a cup of tea... We do have to be mindful that we don't use food to manage feelings as that can lead to an unhealthy relationship with food into adulthood, using food for comfort. While I don't think it is necessarily a bad thing to continue to use a cup of tea as the answer for everything, baking has had an interesting effect on giving the children the chance to feel disappointment when our cakes, biscuits or pastries didn't quite turn out the way we had hoped. This also built resilience, determination and figuring out what went wrong and trying again.

As I mentioned in the above section, when children play together in the role play kitchen or mud kitchen, they start to figure out what to do when they don't agree on something. For parents, and even as a nanny sometimes, it can be tempting to try and solve the conflict for them, but it is a necessary process children have to go through. Being able to figure out how to overcome a disagreement in a way that solves the problem for everyone will see them through in later life. If someone else wants the fancy blue cup, and snatches it, they may feel indignant, and of course, if they ask for your input or if the solution becomes physical, you need to be involved, but it's much more beneficial to watch what happens and then verbally reward them for resolving conflict. Forcing a sorry doesn't work ever and before 4-years-old, children struggle to feel empathy anyway. Turn taking, sharing, thinking about how other people feel can all develop through role play.

Mealtimes can provide an even better way to manage feelings. Feeling belonging, feeling heard, forming stronger bonds with siblings and parents... all of this happens best around the kitchen or dining table. I appreciate life is busy, I understand that you might not want to eat at 5 when the children are hungry, but the benefits outweigh all of that. Not only do studies from the National Institute of Health (2021) and the Department of Education (2008/2015) talk about how children eat more fruits and vegetables when the family sits at the table, but their overall well-being improves too because of the social interactions.

Actions

***make a mud pie or leaf soup, post it on Instagram tagging @more_to_organising #moretomealtimes #mudpie #leafsoup**

***commit to eating together at the table**

Literacy

Phonics

"When your spelling homework words become cake decorations and your Tupperware cupboards have never looked so organised, Kat is around." (Aly, Kew).

One of my favourite things to do is turn one activity into another, and using icing to write digraphs, trigraphs, tricky words and High Frequency words definitely makes the spelling homework more memorable for the children. More phonics will be talked about in the section below.

Mark Making and Writing Opportunities

Shopping Lists

The reason I love to store items in see-through containers is because it is immediately obvious what is running low. This way, the children can be involved in thinking about what needs to be replenished. Providing a notepad and pencil means they can mark-make for a purpose. Your children do not have to be great at phonics to be involved in writing a shopping list. Start with letting them draw the items, you can annotate for them. Then progress to drawing and writing the word onset sound, developing into sounding out the whole words as they develop. With my current family, we have a magnetic white board on the fridge, when items run low, I write them on the white board, so the parents know to add it to the order. The children have started to add things there too.

Recipes

If there is a recipe that the children love to eat, why not create a recipe booklet of all your favourite dishes and add as you go along? Many recipes are online these days, and while you can look them up again, it is not guaranteed that you will find the same one. Also, as I believe cooking is an art, the great thing is you can be creative with the recipes, adding in different ingredients and leaving out ones they are not so keen on. There are formats on twinkl.com but you can easily use plain paper, let the children create a border and draw the ingredients or pictures around the outside. Being able to write non- fiction texts for a purpose is a great skill: writing lists, using imperative verbs (bossy verbs), numbering steps, ordering steps and time conjunctions.

Menus

During the Pandemic, we often made food for the whole family. A special treat was making a party tea for no other reason than we were all in the house. For this, the then 8-year-old wrote a shopping list for what we needed and then when we made all the food items; she also made a menu for her mum, stepdad, and sister to choose what they would like so she could serve them. She would hand write a menu for everyone in the family. On her Menus, she included starters, mains, desserts, as well as drink options, meaning she had to use titles and subtitles. She could get creative in describing the dishes using expanded noun phrases to make the meal more enticing.

I think the writing is even better when the food is real, the purpose behind the activity is also real.

<u>Taking Orders</u>

With the example above, the 8-year-old also took her family's orders and wrote them down. Taking notes is a skill. Again, there is a real purpose behind the activity.

Having a play kitchen opens the doors to so many role play opportunities. Children can, of course, play making homes, but I have found they also love to play restaurants. I once went on a 'date' with Mr. Potato Head while the 7-year-old and the 5-year-old took our order. I was a bit worried when they served chips to him, but he didn't seem to mind!

<u>Reading</u>

One of the compliments I get from my Organising clients is that they love that I place appropriate books in the areas of the playrooms I sort, so the children always have access to reading opportunities. Within your kitchen role play areas, add in recipe books, as well as menus, written shopping lists, adverts or leaflets for local farms/farm shops or new restaurants.

As well as this, explore books through food or food through books. In this section, I am going to share my favourite children's books that have food or meals in them. Many of these have been loved by my nanny children too. This is a crossover with '*There's More to Books than Reading*', my first book. You really will bring stories to life if you make the food in the books.

This list is not exhaustive. Please enjoy lots of books and try lots of foods!

Avocado Baby by John Burningham

As all parents do, they want their baby to grow up big and strong, but their child won't eat anything until one day, he finds an avocado in the fruit bowl and eats it all up. He does indeed get very strong. Add avocado into your smoothies, mash it up to have on toast, or make slices and enjoy.

The Runaway Pea by Kjartan Poskitt and illustrated by Alex Wilmore

Peas always end up on the floor. We have a running joke of, "Somebody pea'd on the floor," but this is a great book to read while you're eating your peas. Oh, and don't forget to check under the fridge for your runaway peas!

Supertato by Sue Hendra

We read this whole series during bath time! One of our routines is that the children get to choose a book or choose a song for bath time. It gets them in the bath with minimal effort. Along with the evil pea, and the melting ice lollies, there is much fun to be had. Why not see if you can eat all the fruits and vegetables in the book – probably not in the bath though!

Handa's Surprise by Eileen Browne

Handa takes gorgeous tropical fruits to her friend, but little does she know, animals are replacing all the different fruits as she walks past, so when she gets to her friends, she is also surprised! This is great for helping you on 'Try- It Tuesdays,' and will help you learn about fruit from different countries together. Check out the section on Understanding the World- People and Communities for more ideas on how to use food to help our children learn about other cultures.

I will not ever never eat a tomato by Lauren Child

I actually met Lauren Child and she gave me a direct quote for my first book about her favourite book that she had loved as a child and what book she loved to read to her own children. If you want to know what she said (and others, such as Charlaine Harris who wrote Trueblood and Dom Joly from Trigger Happy TV) head to www.moretoorganising.com and click on the Amazon link or contact me for a personalised signed copy. I have used this book in workshops in nurseries several times.

Firstly, Lola says she won't eat anything... Remember, it is ok to have preferences - Don't yum my yuk! Lola is encouraged to try new foods through imaginative persuasion, which is great for nurturing an environment where your own children will learn to try and retry new foods. Not only can you make a whole meal from this book, with fluffy clouds from Mount

Fuji, green drops from Greenland, moon squirters, ocean nibbles and orange twiglets from Jupiter, but I also use the foods in this book to talk about different shapes.

Stone Soup by Tony Ross

I did this with a class when I was a teacher. It is a great one to do with actual food. Obviously, don't put the stone in the pan. It is actually a folktale which dates as far back as 1720 in France. The message in it is one of sharing. Strangers convince the villagers to share small amounts of their food and put it in the soup. Eventually, they have a wonderful soup that everyone can enjoy.

The Runaway Chapati by Susan Price

Again, using books to help us learn about other cultures or religions, this book is similar to The Runaway Gingerbread Man. So why not read both and make chapatis and decorate some gingerbreads?

The Enormous Turnip by Katie Daynes

I also used this book when I was teaching science. We were thinking about pushing and pulling. The turnip is so big, they need everyone to come and help them pull it out of the ground. It would also be a great book to read for when you visit the pick your own farm and maybe do your own turnip pulling.

Actions

***involve the children in writing the shopping list- post on Instagram tagging @more_to_organising with the hashtags #moretomealtimes #shoppinglist**

***start making a family recipe book of your favourite meals. Share your best one on Instagram, tagging @more_to_organising with the hashtags #moretomealtimes #recipes**

***make a café with real food for a meal, post pictures of the menus, orders and tables tagging @more_to_organising with the hashtags #moretomealtimes #menus #caferoleplay**

Physical Development

Health and Well-being

The first part of this section is not very pleasant, so I am going to preface it with a Trigger Warning- cuts, burns, choking, death. It could be renamed the First Aid Chapter.

The most obvious health benefits children get from learning about how to fuel their bodies is learning to eat foods in a balanced way. But in the spirit of the title of this book, there is more to it than that. You need to know all about the risks which in turn include moving and handling. There is a Moving and Handling overlap here, but for the interest of looking at this from a health and safety perspective, I will explain all the reasons why it is so important for our children to practise these skills before they even apply it to food stuffs; try things out in a safe environment with an adult present and crucially, learning what to do if something does go wrong too. I have been doing my Paediatric first aid every three years since I started teaching, and not to show my age, but if you can work out the maths, I have 7 paediatric First Aid certificates at the time of writing. In that time, I have experienced having to use my knowledge and skills and have heard lots of horrible stories of when things went wrong. Whilst I don't want to scare you or worry you, prevention is so much better than cure, and cure is the wrong word here, because sometimes mistakes made in the kitchen can lead to lifelong scars or worse, death. So, on that cheery note, I am going to tell you a success story…

One of my first travel jobs was working on a cruise ship for a billionaire. The little boy I was looking after had just turned 4 (he had an older brother, but I didn't look after him) and I also often looked after his best friend who was 6. This wasn't a normal family trip because my children's parents invited 50 of their closest friends and family, and two nannies; I was one of them. Now, I don't know if you've tried to check in on a cruise ship with just a family of 4 but checking in 50 people takes a little longer, meaning there was a lot of waiting around. I will premise this next part with, I should have been firmer, shouted louder, been stronger; I am definitely all of those things now. The parents and aunts were all around with me and the children. All the children were running around and at some point, asked for a snack. One of the aunts gave my 4-year-old an apple, to which I said, "Sit down while you're eating." You can guess what is coming. I was a young nanny, I am not making excuses, let's face it, this could have been the end of my career. There were so many other adults around who were related to the child, all the other children were running around, and I repeated myself. It was my second day in this job, the children weren't listening, I was not being strong enough and the adults were going against me, saying I should let them be. He choked. I have no idea what took over me, but I felt like I had been a robot after the fact. I lost all emotion and just went into the back blows straight away from where he was standing. The aunts told me I was an angel after that, but it could have been prevented. I promise you, I have never and will never allow that situation to occur again. The one thing that prevented the situation from being much worse was that I hadn't taken my eye off him for even a moment. The act of choking can be silent.

If you have done a first aid course you might have heard this next story, but especially in posh restaurants, when adults feel like they are choking, they go into the toilets so as not to make a fuss. There are sadly many instances of people dying because of doing this. The signs of someone choking are: not being able to make a noise or cough, difficulty breathing, blue lips and eventually unconsciousness. I feel so strongly about making children aware of the dangers of choking. Even before children can talk, getting into the habit of only eating while sitting down will prevent a lot of chokings. When they can understand you more, I talk about the size of the food and the size of their throat. You can show them by creating a circle out of your thumb and finger. Try pushing a grape through the hole, then quarter the grape lengthways and show them again. There needs to be space at each side to let air through. Making something like this very visual really helps them to understand. It is no good saying, "You can't eat that, you might choke," as choking is arbitrary. Tell them that the food item is exactly the same size as their throat, and it can get stuck. If it gets stuck, you can't breathe. We need to breathe to keep all the other things in our bodies working, like our brain sending messages to the rest of our bodies, or our hearts pumping blood around our body. Foods that people often don't think about are sausages and popcorn. Sausages can be sliced in half long ways and then cut into small pieces whereas popcorn is just a hazard.

I am going to shock you now. At what age should you stop cutting the grapes into length way quarters? A lot of people say when they are no longer a toddler. A lot of people say when they have left nursery. It is actually aged 5. I currently look after a 5-year-old and generally still halve her grapes, but she wants to be grown up like her elder siblings. To get over this, I either just slice them all in half and then no one is different, or I sit next to her and remind her to bite it as soon as it hits her mouth, that way, it is halved before it enters. I suppose I am scarred by the experience with the 4-year-old on the cruise ship. But I will never not be vigilant about this.

I also teach my children what to do if they do choke. As it is a silent killer, I tell them to knock over their cup, bang something or grab my hand if in reach. This is another reason why it is so important to sit at the table with your children when they are eating. If you make them aware that this is ok, when it does happen, look at them first and not the mess. When something falls over, we generally look at where the noise came from. The faster you can act, the more likely our children are to survive.

And for all the adults reading who are now worried about themselves, if you are alone, they say run into a chair as this acts as a blow under your diaphragm and can push the offending article out. Please don't go into a restaurant bathroom alone. I also prepare the children in case something happens to me when I am looking after them alone, as accidents can occur in the kitchen or anywhere. I show them how to access my phone for the emergency services and make sure they know where they live when they are of speaking age.

Another awful story when it comes to First Aid, or rather preventing the need for First Aid, involves boiling water. I was talking about this book to a friend, and she said when her brother was little, he accidentally pulled a cup of tea over him, which caused lifelong burns. Making sure cups of tea are unreachable, turning the pan handles in on the hob (or stove) and only letting them pour boiling water when you have absolutely made sure they can pour confidently can reduce this, but let's face it, even adults make faux pas. Hands up if you've ever had a burn! (Raises own hand) I know all the hazards. I have literally passed qualifications every three years for the last 18 years. I genuinely believe we should give children basic first aid knowledge as soon as possible. If you get a first-degree burn, putting it under cold running water can alleviate the pain. Putting it in a bowl of cold water will only heat the water up. How long should you run it under the tap? A lot longer than we do generally.

Using blunt knives causes more accidents than sharp knives as sharp knives cut through the intended vegetable or food item easily. If children have already been practising on their playdough, and they are cutting in a safe environment, knowing all the risks, they are more likely to be successfully sensible or sensibly successful. It is elderly people, according to one of my many First Aid Teachers, that end up in hospital for trying to cut something with a blunt knife. If the knife cannot cut smoothly, it's more likely to slip and cut something unintended, such as a finger. You know another ridiculously sharp thing? Tin lids. One thing that I am still wary of letting any children do is opening tins. It is not even that the ring pull system isn't efficient. I just moved a tuna tin once and sliced my finger. The worry with that is the possibility of infection. Cutting yourself on a clean knife is bad, but not as bad as cutting it on a fishy slice. There are tin openers that, depending on the way you use them, the lid is quite safe, and it's just the top of the tin that is sharp, which means accidents can be more easily avoided. So, again, this is something to be practised with you there, with lots of modelling and guiding.

What is the worst fruit to cut? What is the one that sends the most people to the hospital? Because I have called it a fruit, it might have thrown you off a bit. It is actually a salad item. And I have been told to eat more of them to up my good cholesterol. Were you listening? It's the avocado pear! People hold them in their hand and slice, cutting their palm as well as the Avo. Recently, I have even had the stone fly off my cutting board, and I am a sensible avocado cutting person. So, approach with caution. Depending on the depth of the cut, you might need to go to hospital, but teaching our children to stop the bleeding by raising it up, only applying pressure if the wound does not have anything stuck in it, add antiseptic, and cover with a clean bandage. I really would encourage you to do a first aid certificate if you haven't got one. I had one nanny family whose parents did take one, and they were so enlightened. There were so many things that they didn't know. The key message I want you to take away from this part of the chapter is not to wrap your children in cotton wool, thereby preventing them from learning all the skills they need for their future, but to empower them, to guide them safely and let them be aware of all the risks.

Dissolving is something we can cover in science as well as health. I think most of us are really good at teaching our children to get into the habit of cleaning their teeth, but there are more ways that we can empower our children to take care of their teeth. When my brother was a teenager, the dentist told him that he had to stop drinking fizzy pop. He would have 2 litre bottles in his room and just chug all day. I think the worst thing about drinks when we were teens is that unhealthy drinks were marketed as healthy for you such as Sunny D. The good old clean a penny with cola stills shows what it is doing to our teeth or our insides. Replacing these drinks with ones that purport to be better for you such as diet drinks can be misleading as these are full of aspartame which is an artificial sweetener and not especially healthy. At university, I started drinking diet coke every day and it did affect my bowel movements, or lack of, to put it as politely as possible. So, as with everything in this book, I think it should be met with balance. Not like my brother in his teens, and not like me at university.

I was talking to some nannies about this part of the book, and one said that she knew of a child that needed 5 teeth taken out at 9 which is heart-breaking. These were her adult teeth that she'd only had for a few years. When I was about to train to be a teacher at Durham University, they asked you to spend two weeks in a primary school, in every year group. I went to a lovely school in Todmorden. In the reception, there were children who just had little black stumps in their mouths instead of teeth. It is only recently in my life that I have found out that you are not supposed to clean your teeth after breakfast. I used to eat breakfast and then brush my teeth right before I left the house. Eating a breakfast that is very sugary or acidic weakens the enamel and brushing straight after eating can cause even more damage.

Actions

***show the children the grape/throat size activity talked about in the last section**

***do a first aid certificate**

***buy purple teeth tablets to get even better at cleaning your teeth, do it with your children**

Well-being

On to nicer things, let's talk about well- being. There are certain foods that give our hormones a boost. When we know about these, when we are feeling not ourselves, we can use them as tools to help us.

I spoke in the introduction about my own use of food for comfort. While bingeing on cake and biscuits might give me a small boost in that moment, in the long run, it doesn't enhance my well-being. I inevitably feel rubbish the next day, or even straight after.

I have had such a kick out of adding salmon, avocado and dark chocolate into my meal plans. Not only does it mean I have been replacing other foods I might have chosen, but the nurse also said that eating these foods would make me feel less lethargic. Eating to fuel our bodies and minds is the greatest way to support our mental health. As I have mentioned, I am a marathon runner, and while I get a huge boost when running, known as the runners high, what we put in our bodies has more of an impact on our health than exercise does.

In my second book, I talk about decluttering, and here is no different. But what I am asking you to declutter is your words. Bikini bodies, diets, trying to lose a pound, wanting to lose a dress size, being negative about your own body or anyone else's is no longer in your vocabulary. It always makes me cringe when someone says something like that in front of the children, and I will always model back, that I am proud of my strong legs that help me run marathons or how the muscles in my arms mean I can pick up a child. Talking about how fibre helps us poo, calcium makes our bones, teeth, and nails strong, and vitamins help so many things, is much more productive than attaching self-worth onto a number on the scales. The thing is, our children are watching, listening, and copying us. Being mindful about this can help them not to follow in our negative footsteps.

As mentioned in the managing feelings section, having meals together because of the social interactions, had a positive impact on the children I've worked with overall.

Speaking of well-being, getting into the habit of yoga has so many benefits. While in the next section, I will be talking about how we can improve moving and handling, gross and fine motor skills through learning about food, here is where exercise is beneficial for digestion. Having the correct posture when we eat not only reduces the risk of choking, but it also actually enhances how our body processes food.

Moving and Handling

As with getting children involved, there are certain fine motor skills that need to be developed, you can do these with the foods and liquids, but they can also practise these skills within their play. Pouring liquids into the bath helps them with their hand- eye coordination. During the summer, using jugs in the paddling pool also uses these skills. If you never let your children pour water into their cup, they will never be able to do it. If doing it at the table, start with less water in the jug so it is not too heavy, whereas in water play, they can experiment with how much water they can fill, carry, and pour. By doing this in an experimental setting where it is ok to spill, they learn what they are capable of and so, when it does come to pouring at the table, they are more likely to achieve the desired outcome. If they do spill, how you react is very important. I talk about learned helplessness a lot in my workshop on resilience. If a child feels like they can't do something, and when they try an adult takes over and does it for them, they will learn that they are either not good enough to do it or worse, decide not to try because they know you will do it for them if they wait long enough. Creating a space where it is ok to make mistakes is the first building block to instilling confidence and developing their positive self- esteem.

Playdough

As with pouring, before you even get to using a cutter or a knife on foods, playdough is an amazing way to practise all those amazing fine motor skills. Playdough also helps us with so much more. Head to twinkl.com to find all the different recipes you can make. My favourites are the 'no cook' ones. You can experiment with colours and scents. Your children can practise all the skills needed with malleable resources- kneading, rolling, squishing. Have fun with it together. I have had amazing role play experiences with children, where they make things and put them in their role play ovens. We've also made price lists and got the pretend money out. Making cubes from a ball and turning them into dice transformed our play into a maths activity where we rolled our home-made dice and added the dots. The possibilities are endless. Get over not letting them mix the colours. This is part of play. Making your own playdough means the expense isn't as great, although in my experience, it does go mouldy, so swings and roundabouts. Keep it in a Tupperware box to make it last a little longer.

Gross Motor skills - In the section on getting children involved, I talk about 'pick your own farms'. In the experiences we have had, children have used pitchforks to dig up carrots, hand shovels to uncover potatoes, and I have seen them use their whole bodies to pick up pumpkins, courgettes and marrows that were bigger than their bodies. When I first started working at Marks and Spencer's food, we had to have training on how to pick up heavy boxes to protect our backs against slipped discs. It occurred to my 20-year-old self, that I had been picking up children heavier than some of the boxes for years already. Modelling how to pick up those pumpkins, by bending your knees and pulling up through your thighs, rather than bending at the hips, is much better for our backs. Why not teach that skill from an early age? Yes, they are more flexible than us, and I know we have talked about sensible risks before, but sometimes, they want to try to do things for themselves. For some reason, children have much more self-belief in carrying something that we perceive as far too heavy than other tasks that they can probably achieve with much less effort. I will give you a non-food example. Sticks. Or rather branches. I once tried to write a children's book on all the reasons why dogs and toddlers are similar, and this is one of them. Have you ever seen a dog pootle along the riverside with a stick that takes up the whole path? If you haven't, it is quite the sight to behold. The dogs are usually a fraction of the size of the, let's face it, branch, not stick. They are also usually the happiest dogs on the path. It is the same with children. The bigger the stick, the happier they seem to be. Which means they need to know how to pick it up, they need to know about balance and coordination, which are also gross motor skills. So let them pick up the branches but talk about being mindful of others in the park and talk about keeping them below eye level so we prevent unnecessary poking incidents and prepare them for when they want to pick up that pumpkin for Halloween or the marrow for tea. Again, they will need to use their gross motor skills to do the picking up, but to carry it to the car, they will need their balancing and coordination skills. Add to that, that the fields these vegetables grow in (or fruits because they have seeds), are usually undulated. It's just all round a fantastic experience for them (and us). I will talk about Pick Your Own Farms again in the measurement section.

Actions

***change how you speak about your own body**

***let children pour their own water**

***go back to the Pick Your Own Farm and share on Instagram tagging @more_to_organising with the hashtags #moretomealtimes #pickyourown**

***practise all the skills for prepping with playdough (you play with it too)**

Maths

I know I am not the only one that will tell you that cooking is wonderful for our children's mathematical skills. It is probably really obvious, but I think some of the things I am going to discuss might not be so obvious. I am also going to talk further about how to differentiate these skills as I have always had different ages of siblings, but even if you only have one child, what you do when they are 2 will change when they become 5, and as I have mentioned, it isn't necessarily age-related, these tasks are developmentally appropriate. In all honesty, I could go through these steps with my dad, who knows the basics and I think, low-key, enjoys it when we bake together but honestly, doesn't have a clue on baking. Many times, when I go to see him, he has pulled out a recipe from a magazine that he would quite like to eat. One standout one for me was a rhubarb cake crumble. He grows rhubarb in his garden so always has an abundance. While stewing it and eating it with custard suffices him, when I am around, we create things a little more exciting. A cake crumble was different for me. I can easily make cake batter. Crumble is ok, but I do believe there is more skill to that, but to make a cake crumble, this was an adventure even for me. I think that's why I do want the message of this book to get far and wide. I want the next generation to plunge in and find all learning, all challenges, all new things to be exciting and something that they want to overcome. Not have to wait for their daughter to visit or rely on someone else, or have to buy a processed rhubarb crumble, meaning they still have an abundance of great produce to eat in some other way.

Numbers

Looking at recipes, there will be numbers throughout the book. Using the contents page and index page to find the correct page number, not only is a skill for reading non-fiction texts, but also helps with number recognition. Within the ingredients, there will be numbers of grams or litres etc.

Then even the instructions will have numbered steps. These are all practical reasons your children need to be able to recognise numbers for their development. I don't like worksheets and I am even against homework as children and adults don't always know the purpose of the activity. Looking at recipes means you can explore numbers together – without a worksheet - and then baking and cooking means they can use their skills in real life.

Counting

Setting the table lends itself to counting. How many plates do we need? How many spoons do we need? Can they use the cutter to make 5 heart cucumbers?

In the Early Years Foundation stage, we encourage children to understand one- to- one correspondence by physically moving an object; once they have understood 3, move to 5, then 10. Eventually, you can ask them to count how many peas they have using this method.

Addition and Subtraction

Visually practising addition with the added kinaesthetic (moving the carrot pieces), really cements the learning. If they have 3 carrot sticks and they can have 4 more, they can add it. The best thing is, when we are taking away, we get to eat the object. When we 'take away' objects, they haven't really gone anywhere, sure, you can move them to a different part of the table, but the physical act of eating definitely takes them away. When I do subtraction at the beginning, without food, I encourage them to 'eat' their fingers. Don't worry, they know to not actually eat their fingers, but this action means more to them than just putting a finger down in the first instance. Also, it is a little fun. So, when they are doing subtraction without their carrot sticks, they still have formed that memory to be able to do it themselves.

We often count how many different fruits and vegetables we have had that day. When I was little, they used to say we should eat five portions of fruit or vegetables a day which I do believe has gone up to seven. Personally, I wouldn't restrict children like that, but providing at least one fruit or vegetable for every meal and snack, you could easily get to at least 8. Breakfast, morning snack, dinner, afternoon snack and tea. Also, they might have 10 blueberries for morning snack, 20 peas at dinner, 3 broccoli trees at teatime, 8 strawberries after tea, you get the picture. Now this shouldn't be laborious. I am not saying force them to count how many they have every day, but you could have competitions to see if they can eat more than they did before every now and again.

Times Tables

To differentiate counting for learners that need something more developmentally appropriate, ask them how many they need in total. For example, if you have three siblings and two parents, that is 5 people and everyone gets 5 carrot sticks, let's pretend. You can start introducing this as a concept by placing the carrot sticks on five plates, then they count in 5's. You can change the numbers to create different sums to make it harder. With the 3 siblings, they get 6 strawberries each. Suddenly, you have differentiated the task. You have changed the difficulty appropriately for the level of the other siblings. You're doing the same task. You are all learning times tables. Eventually, you can say, how many tomatoes do we need to take out, wash, and share if we have 4 each? This helps the children to practise doing calculations in their head.

You can also do this with teddies and pretend food in the role play kitchen.

In my first blog, www.moretobooks.blog, there is an idea for fruit pastille maths. The children loved it.

Division/sharing

Arrays are tables where there are rows across and rows down which correlate to the total number. I have done this with tins in an interview for a school in Year 2. We made vertical arrays stacking the tins on top of each other. For example, I have 15 tins but only three shelves, how many can fit on each shelf? This is not only visual but also physical. The children would stack three tins, then move onto the next 'row until they used all 15 tins. They would end up with 5 stacks. So, 15 divided by 3 is 5. Applying this activity to your mealtimes, is a fun way to practise division. Remember to keep the balance, food needn't be solely about eating fruits and vegetables, it is about yin and yang, it's about creating young adults who can be mindful and successful So, with that in mind, if you have 27 mini marshmallows for our hot chocolates and three siblings, can they physically put the marshmallows onto the cream, to find that 27 divided by 3 is 9?

I switch the words 'dividing' and 'sharing' interchangeably throughout the tasks. When their teacher does inevitably send that unpurposeful worksheet for homework, and it says divide these, they'll be able to say, "We did this with marshmallows, it was so fun, and I am confident I know what to do!" Saying that, you can't just do an activity once and expect children to understand straight away. Remember, if I asked you to play the flute, I wouldn't expect you to get a song perfect, and apply your knowledge to a different tune, without some practice. So go ahead and do your sharing with the marshmallows, but also apply it to the blueberries dropped into yogurts and their chicken nuggets for tea; (we make home-made ones but remember, if you need a frozen food day, it's about balance - not all the time cooking from scratch, not all the time eating processed food).

Measures

I think weighing items and pouring liquids is what everyone thinks of when we talk about cooking and baking as being great for mathematical development, but we can also look at time and temperature.

To differentiate, first, you would just start to use the vocabulary around weight and size. We will mention this again in the section on Shape. When holding an apple or a melon, one is heavier/bigger than the other. It is important to note, just because something is bigger doesn't mean it is heavier, think candy floss (remember, it's about balance).

Even on a private island off the coast of Mozambique when I was a travel nanny, having a 'picnic' which was at a table, with chairs and a gazebo that had been brought to the remote beach, our carrot sticks were still all different sizes, and whilst we didn't weigh them, we did order them in size from shortest to longest, (if we weren't on a remote beach, we could have measured them with a ruler). So, wherever you are, there is opportunity for learning.

Weight

I am always bemused by my American bosses when they bring out the cups to measure flour. While I can't deny that it is quicker and easier for learning, I don't think it helps our children get the concept of what something weighs. When I was a teenager, I started to come across recipes with cups in them. I didn't think to ask what that meant, I just used a regular cup. Like a mug! I think because the ratios of the ingredients were still similar, it generally worked out ok. It wasn't until I had my first role with an American family that I realised that measuring 'cups' were actual things you could buy. It is quite a fun activity to estimate what a food item will weigh, and then let the children put it on a weighing scale. They could even compare it to a bag of flour. Like with the adding up of all the fruits and vegetables, don't make it laborious. It is not that you do this every day. In fact, just introducing it as a game one time will probably pique their interest to do it more than once so it becomes intrinsic.

When baking, to differentiate, I will begin by model pouring out the flour onto the scale. I will write the number we are trying to get to and ask the child to help me get the correct number; when the number on the scale matches the number written, they let me know. That way, they are still involved. This links to their physical development. While it doesn't matter if they try and weigh it out, get it wrong and we make a big mess, without modelling how to do it, it may take longer to get the desired outcome. We will talk about trying not to waste food in the chapter on Sustainability, but it is all a learning curve. Model it, let them practise, model again, let them improve. They probably won't get it straight away and that's ok. They might not get it the third or fourth time without spilling, but one thing I know for sure, is if we never let them try, they will never improve.

The next step would be to verbally talk about the number of grams we need and let them do it for themselves. You will have modelled in the first instance that you don't just pour it crazily, but you pour to about 80% and then go slower by the end so as not to go too far over. It is ok for them to go over a little, and you probably will yourself. Side note, how great does it feel when you get right on the dot? I haven't had a car for a long time, but that's another time when I feel amazing for getting the measure just right – getting the fuel counter to the exact penny! Always having a clean teaspoon nearby, means they can rectify if they do go a little over. This is practising subtraction in a purposeful way.

The last step would be to not talk about how much they need at all. They are totally independent, read the recipe and pour it themselves. This is where we want to get them ultimately.

Part of measuring also involves liquids. As we have said, children can practise their physical skills by using jugs in the bath. More than just pouring water out and learning to control the jug, start to look at the numbers on the jug. If the weather is nice, put jugs in the paddling pool and start to talk about millilitres and litres. When they are making their natural noodle 'soups' in the mud kitchen with leaves, petals and twigs, use language relating to measurements.

Temperature

The basics in temperature are for safety. Has a child ever tried their food that was too hot and then asked you why you didn't tell them? That happened to me last year. Every day, I would say, "Be careful, blow on it, it's hot," and this one time I didn't. My youngest just ploughed in and then found out it was too hot. Don't worry, we had water on the table and there was no lasting damage. But it was a good learning curve for me. I had assumed that she would know it was hot because all the other days it was hot! So, I started saying, "Watch out, it's just come out of the freezer," and the children would reply with giggles because they had seen it come out of the oven.

The other times temperature is for safety is when we think about the oven, hob/stove being on. Things being too hot means burns.

We also need to talk about the other extreme. When we are making our ice lollies, we need things to be freezing cold. To keep food from growing bacteria, we need them to be cold. This is the beginning of learning about temperature. Just start using the vocabulary relating to different temperatures and why this might be important. This learning crosses over to science topics such as solids, liquids, and gases.

Our recipes will all require different temperatures. I think when people think of teaching measurements, degrees seem to not be taught as much. Look at all the recipes and talk about the different temperatures needed for different meals. Let them turn the dial on the oven to get the correct temperature and talk about the fact that it takes time to get to that temperature. A lot of these things might sound so obvious. If you have an air fryer for example, you still need to set the temperature. You just adjust the amount of time you cook.

Time

Going back to the recipes, when we look at instructions, they will talk about minutes and hours. This is a perfect way to practise time skills in a purposeful way. It can be tempting just to ask Alexa to put a timer on for however long it takes, and I have done that. But I also encourage the children to put a timer on the oven. This means they are connecting the minutes to the number in the recipe. Even without a recipe, children love to put the timer on. They can also check this by pressing to see how long is left. This is using subtraction in a meaningful way. On top of this, I would look at an analogue clock too. Tell them, we put it in the oven at 5 o'clock and it will take around half an hour, so when the big hand points to 6, that will be half past, which is 30 minutes.

I am going to talk more about batch cooking, freezing, refrigerating, and re-using leftovers in the chapter on sustainability, but in terms of this section, I think it is important to talk about how long things can be kept in the fridge or how long they can be kept in the freezer etc. Not only can this knowledge help our planet by using up food and not letting it go into landfill, but we can also learn about hours, days, months etc. Putting the date on the items that you put it in the freezer is the bare minimum - as well as writing what is in the container. I have had a few mishaps with unlabelled Tupperware before I became a Professional Organiser. I once almost mixed a pasta Bolognese portion with a tuna pasta bake much to the children's disgust! We have also had chorizo pasta sauce unlabelled which led to upset as one child really didn't like chorizo, and there are only so many days plain pasta with butter counts as a meal. I know you will understand what I mean by that!

Produce that is meant to be kept in the fridge but has been left out, has only a finite time before bacteria grows. After 4 hours, it should be binned. This has an impact on when you buy your shopping and how long it takes to get home. This also has an impact on when you pack a lunch and plan to eat it. All this should be an open conversation with our children.

Dried foods can be kept for months, and tinned foods may be kept for years. This is a great opportunity to talk about dates in a purposeful way. I talk about this in the section about getting children involved, pulling out all your tins and checking dates means they are involved in knowing what is in the cupboards, what you are running low on, what you need to add to the shopping list, and also what you really don't like to eat. If you have tins that are past their best, you need to add them to your meal plan (which you also involve the children in) or you accept that you don't like that food, and it is taking up valuable space in your home.

I think of things like this, if food is in the fridge- days or weeks, and if it's in the freezer, months. I also do an audit of my freezer quarterly, as although it is very small, when I do batch cook, I plan it into my meal plan, meaning other foods can get left to the end. It may not even be that I don't like them, it is just that I love other foods more, so they tend to be used up first. We all get into ruts so it's good to shake things up a bit. I did an experiment with my clothes once. I wasn't allowed to wear something again without wearing all the other items first. I have my favourite running top and my favourite trousers etc, so it soon became really clear which clothes I just do not wear. When I did the same thing for my food, it was a bit psychologically unnerving to end up with almost bare cupboards and an almost bare fridge, but what it really showed me was what foods I gravitated to the most, and by the end of the experiment, I had some really odd concoctions for sure! The reason I wanted to do this food audit is because we can waste so much money buying more shopping when we still have perfectly good food just slowly going past its best. I have felt the bare cupboards before…

When I was at university, I was staying in the University house alone for the four weeks at Easter. I did have a job at a pub where I was a runner (I took the food from the kitchen to the table) but I had two weeks where I had no money. I am not talking 'no money' but still managed to go shopping, not 'no money' but enough to meet friends for drinks, I mean there was not one penny to buy anything. I had just enough petrol in the tank to get to work and back, and thankfully, they provided a meal if I worked a shift over a certain number of hours. What I did have in my freezer was onion rings, so I had some meals of just onion rings, and I also had pasta, tinned tuna and tinned tomatoes and a block of cheese in my fridge. I made a huge tuna pasta bake and kept it in the oven…for a week! I am so surprised that I didn't get really sick. I suppose the only thing I should be thankful for is that I couldn't afford to put the heating on, so the kitchen probably acted as a fridge. After doing my food hygiene learning within my nutrition for children course, I realised how bad that could have been. I don't know why it didn't occur to me to spoon it into bowls and pop them in the fridge.

So, let's make sure our children know how to stay healthy, make food and store it safely so they don't do what I did.

Money

Part of the meal planning process can help our children think about how much things cost and whilst I appreciate some families don't have to think about money as much as others, but consider if they go to university, or when they move into their first home, be it with a partner or friends. Budgeting is something that everyone needs to do no matter how much money they have, it may just be on a different scale. The craziest thing about today's economy or society for me, is that it is actually cheaper for me to eat at a restaurant than it is to get takeaway in London, as a person living on my own.

The way to get the most from your money is to plan what you want to eat, cook from scratch, make batches, and make sure you eat it before it goes off.

One of the most interesting conversations I have with children is about the times I used to take our dog for a walk when I was little. My mum would sometimes give me £1 to walk the dog to the corner shop, which was a fair enough distance for William to have a good walk, and a further incentive for me. I used to be able to buy 3 chocolate bars and 10 penny sweets with my pound. First of all, the children's minds are blown that any sweet could cost a penny, and I do talk about two penny sweets too, don't worry, but when they have done the mental maths, (which is a three-step problem with subtraction and division in this case), they realise that I got three chocolate bars as well as the sweeties for the same price as one chocolate bar nowadays; minds definitely blown. And that little conversation is the start of talking about inflation!

Giving your child money, actual money, and letting them learn how to spend it in the shop, figuring out what they can buy with that, how much change they will get will set them up better for their future. I had a child in my Year 2 class who couldn't read or write, but he was amazing at money. That was his language. Moving to a cashless society means children don't really understand the value of what the coins mean but it's more than that. Tap, tap, tapping away with our plastic cards makes the transactions meaningless to them. When you pay with a note, it is more obvious that you get less money back than you started with.

I often talk about ha'pennies and thrupennies, not because I have ever seen or used them, but because my dad did. I just find it interesting, and I love looking at Roman coins too. Looking at actual coins, feeling them, understanding them, and using them is how our children will learn best. This is also helping their two-step problem solving skills, as inevitably, they will have to add items up and subtract to find the change.

It can also help with times tables as you can have eight 5 pence pieces, for example.

Shape

Even in terms of toast at breakfast, you can think about shape.

Do they want rectangles, squares, or triangles? As we talk about developmentally appropriate learning, start with 2d shapes, talk about the size of shapes: small, medium, and large and count the sides of the shapes. This can link to music; why not sing about the shapes? When we have rhymes and rhythm, the learning resonates more easily. When they are actually eating the shapes, it is even more memorable.

You can start to use cutters to create different shapes. In my workshops, I give people cheese slices and ask them to cut different shapes out of the cheese. Slices of cheese are really easy to cut. Your children will be able to have fun while learning. I know we were taught not to play with our food, but in this case, they are preparing their own sandwiches. I know they will remember this more than looking at line drawings on a worksheet.

Once you have conquered 2d shapes, start to investigate 3d shapes. Spheres in oranges and cuboid cheese blocks, cubes of carrots and ovoid melons. (That's a 3d oval by the way!)

Marshmallows being cylinders and Ice cream cones being, you guessed it, cones. (Balance) You could even categorise all your foods into 3d shapes. I know

I am saying this again, but don't make it laborious. Make it into a game, do it every now and again. With real life examples, the properties of the shapes will be more obvious. When they see a line drawing on a worksheet at school, they will be able to link it to what they have in their kitchen.

<u>Pattern</u>

Pattern is a mathematical skill. For a barbecue, make meat and vegetable patterns on the kebab stick, or as in the case of the 9-year-old I look after, make blueberry and marshmallow patterns on a stick with a star watermelon at the top. Let them make their own patterns with their own fruit kebabs.

Patterns and designs link to creative development. When decorating cakes or biscuits, they can easily practise patterns.

<u>Ratios</u>

I speak about ice lollies in the section on snacks for summer, but all year round, you can create your own juices by using different ratios of a range of juices. Simplifying it, you can have 1 part concentrate to 4 parts water, with an orange squash for example. Then experiment with flavours, 1 part blackcurrant juice, 1 part orange, 3 parts water…

You can also make ice lollies with individually frozen layers - this takes a bit longer but can be a really nice visual representation of ratios and can provide a great opportunity to talk about time and temperature. (This also means you can talk about time and temperature)

Even baking can be thought of in ratios such as scones are 3 parts flour, 2 parts milk and 1 part fat. The word part looks really weird to me now.

Actions

***find all the numbers in recipe books**

***head to www.moretobooks.blog for Fruit Pastille Maths and Apple Pie Blogs**

***let them write the dates on the labels of your batch cooking and share on Instagram tagging @more_to_organising with the hashtags #moretomealtimes #dates**

***actively involve your children in measuring**

***let your children turn the oven on to the correct temperature stated in recipes**

***use the vocabulary of time when cooking**

***make 2d and 3d shapes when prepping vegetables and fruit, share on Instagram tagging @more_to_organising with the hashtags #moretomealtimes #shapes**

***make a pattern with fruit kebabs, share on Instagram tagging @more_to_organising with the hashtags #moretomealtimes #fruitkebabs**

***experiment with ratios and make different flavoured juices**

Understanding the world

One of my favourite things about travelling is trying new foods that I wouldn't have at home. I believe travel is the best way to understand other cultures, but the great thing is, you can learn about other traditional foods at home.

People and communities in the World

Learning about other communities can be as easy as exploring different recipe books from different countries. You could add these recipes into 'Try- it Tuesdays' or make one day a month where you celebrate everything to do with that place: food, clothes, music, language and famous buildings or people.

With recipe books, there is no need to buy them, just borrow them from the library and then, if you fall in love with the recipes, you can buy the book, or better still, remember your favourite ones in the children's handwritten recipe book.

The great thing about this is you will probably be a learner too. When you are at the library, pick up non-fiction books about the country. Print off the flag of a country and colour it while the food is in the oven. I love using Twinkl.com to help me bring learning to life. They have flags, fact files, PowerPoints. You will know, by now, that I am against worksheets for worksheets sake, which is why the PowerPoints can be great here. You wouldn't have to print out the flags if your children can draw them themselves, but you could make a book, to go with your recipe book of all the things you found out as a family. Twinkl.com also has resources for recipes around the world. I tend to talk a lot about diversity within books, resources, and screen time we provide for our children, and this should extend to foods as well. The reason we should embrace learning about other cultures is to reduce stereotyping and prejudices, support understanding and help our children to be more welcoming of differences.

I like to follow the calendar to help me plan when we learn about some places, for example, every year, I make a big deal out of Chinese New Year. It is one of my most favourite celebrations. CBeebies usually have great videos of children talking about how they celebrate. I find you can learn a lot about other religions by celebrating Eid, Diwali, and Hanukkah. I also use the Christian calendar to inform food choices, for example simnel cake around Mother's Day. I talk about providing a diverse environment in my workshops in homes and nurseries. Using songs will be talked about more in the section on music, for Easter, 'Hot Cross Buns' is a great song to learn while eating hot cross buns for example. It also links to maths with the pennies, and you could look at how much the different kinds of Hot Cross Buns cost now. When I was a child, there was only one kind, but now they have chocolate hot cross buns, they also have cinnamon ones and triple berry ones to name a few.

We can also learn about history through food. So, another day a month, you can choose a time period and find a recipe from that time. Again, Twinkl is great for this. They have recipes for Wartime Trench stew, Great Fire of London Bread, Maya Hot Chocolate, Stone Age Desserts, and Roman Honey biscuits.

Research the calendar together with your children to look for religious festivals but also look out for other events such as Burn's night to maybe try Haggis. There are other days too, such as World Vegetarian Day in October and World Vegan Day in November. There is even National Popcorn Day, National Peanut Butter Day, British Yorkshire Pudding Day and Real Bread Day. The list really is endless, head to www.calendarr.com to see which days are related to food you would like to celebrate. I think I will start to celebrate National Tea Day, oh wait, I think I celebrate that every day!

Actions

***have a Country Celebration- research interesting facts, make a flag and try a traditional dish from that culture. Take photos and share on Instagram tagging @more_to_organising with the hashtags #moretomealtimes #countrycelebration**

***try a dish from history**

***make dishes from Religious Celebrations, you can use the calendar to help you plan when to do this**

***research other celebration days and add them into your menu.**

Technology

I know I talk a lot about using physical recipe books; this takes away from screen time, just as with food intake, we are the children's mentors about creating a healthy balance. I don't think children should never have access to screen time as it is part of our lives now, in fact, they will need technology in some part of their lives, even if it is just online banking and emails. Using the internet to research recipes is a skill. Using apps to order groceries is how a lot of people buy food. Get them involved in this process. These are purposeful screen time activities.

Watch food programmes. While Sunday Kitchen might be boring for them, 'I Can Cook' is brilliant. I looked after a child who loved to watch 'Nailed it' and 'Is it cake?'. I loved to watch 'Junior Bake Off'. There is even a 'MasterChef Junior'. Having other children who inspire them to try new recipes or attempt new techniques can be really impactful. I'll tell you now, the children on these programmes are AMAZING. Children seeing children try, makes them feel like they can try too. It makes me feel like I can do it too. I am not a great cook. I am not a great baker. What I make is edible and I love trying and re-attempting and learning. That's the key for our lifelong learners.

Science

There is no doubt that science happens when we cook, I mentioned this above in the section on temperature. When we freeze liquid, we make solids.

When we heat liquids, they become gases. Children will be able to see the steam coming off their hot foods. When the steam cools again, it turns back into water; children can observe this when you lift the lid on your couscous or rice, as it will be covered in little droplets.

When cooking, children can see irreversible effects by watching things be heated.

Children can learn about dissolving with salt. When I was learning how to cook, my Mum and Grandma taught me to put a pinch of salt in the water for my vegetables, pasta, and rice. When I was teaching my dad to cook a meal, he asked me why I did it. I didn't ever think about why they told me to do that. I suppose I just assumed it might be for flavour, so we looked it up. Learning is about asking questions, being inquisitive and then finding the answer. It does indeed improve the flavour apparently, but it also raises the temperature slightly.

When making peppermint tea, children can learn about absorption with sugar.

This is not food, but one of my favourite experiments is putting flowers in food dye and watching absorption. There are plenty of experiments you can do with food items to learn more about science. Making lava lamps with oil, water, salt, and food colouring in plastic bottles is fun.

Make volcanoes by learning about reactions with mentos and coca cola or baking soda and vinegar.

To start learning about these concepts, just start using the right vocabulary. Ask them what they notice. Get them to ask questions about what is happening. The best way to explore this is to get books on the science of food for children. There are plenty, such as the Kitchen Science cookbook by Dr Michelle Dickenson, Science You Can Eat by Stefan Gates or Edible Science by National Geographic Kids. Alternatively, look experiments up online. Using books means they use less screen time but as mentioned, these are purposeful reasons to use technology.

There is also a lot of science into what our bodies need, and how our food moves through our bodies. One of the ways I do get children to try asparagus and beetroot is to tell them their wee will change and ask them to tell me what difference happens. I had one toddler who ended up loving beetroot after trying it and used to lick it like a lollipop on the end of a fork.

Talking about what colour their wee should be to be healthy helps them in their future. We need to drink enough water for lots of reasons, and while you can talk about measurements of how many litres we should try to drink, another way we can tell is how light in colour our urine is. I don't know a child that doesn't find wee and poo both fascinating and funny. So, bring it in as part of their learning. Looking at their poo after they have eaten sweetcorn can open the conversation about digestion.

The senses are the main thing we can talk about when it comes to food and science - sight, smell, taste, sound, and touch.

Before you even walk in the room, food smells can have your mouth watering. Did you know we can even smell our foods while we are swallowing them? I found that out by reading 'See Inside Your Body' by Katie Daynes and Colin King with the five-year-old I look after. Do you remember one April Fool's Day when they tried to convince us that they would make television into sniffer vision? When I was a teacher, one of the parents gifted me smelly stickers which had all sorts of fruit smells and I even had smelly pencils for my treasure box. You can talk about what foods smell like, you can do smell tests with foods to see which ones you like the most.

As with smell, you can do taste tests. Remember it is ok not to like a food, the only thing is, as our taste buds change, we have to become a little adventurous by trying new foods and also retrying old foods we used to not like. The front of the tongue is more receptive to salty foods, whereas the middle of the tongue can taste sweet things and the back, sour.

We have already talked about how some might not like the feel of raw meat; texture is a huge thing, especially when our children are learning about new foods. Like I said, I don't like the slimy texture of mushrooms and children will have strong reactions to different textures. If our children have sensory issues, it might mean there are more textures they do not want to eat, or they might not like to mix different foods. This is ok. If they will eat them separately, don't try to make things hard for them by forcing them to mix. They still get the nutritional value when the foods are separated, and it might be a more positive experience for them this way. Don't purposely give foods to get a negative reaction, this might mean they stop wanting to try something new. It should be a positive, fun experience.

Whilst what you hear when cooking may not enhance the smells or tastes, the popping of popcorn or the sizzling of sausages is still quite fun. You could talk about what different foods sound like when you bite into them, like the crunch of a carrot, the snap of a cracker, the munch of a biscuit or the chomp of a steak. Even our drinks make sounds like glug, bubble, and fizz. Obviously with children, this is not a great example, but I love the pop of a cork and the glug of wine with a nice meal at the weekend!

Actions

***watch child-friendly cooking programmes**

***conduct a science experiment with food and share on Instagram tagging @more_to_organising with the hashtags #moretomealtimes #scienceexperiments**

Creative development

As I have just done a whole section on science, it cannot be denied that cooking and baking is a science, but I think it is as creative as it is science-y (I know that's not a real word). For sure, in baking there are chemical reactions that occur, and I think the measurements and ratios are important for the best outcome. Those biscuits that say we have to put it in the fridge before cooking do not come out right if you miss that step out and I should know. I have tried. More than once!

The reason I think cooking is somewhat artistic as well as a science, is because I think you can be creative in the ingredients that go together. You can experiment, sciencely (I know this isn't a word either) or creatively, to change the outcome and it doesn't have to be exact. In fact, some people might like things to be spicier than someone else, or you can add just a bit more turmeric to make the colour even brighter. What I am saying is, while the recipes are good guidelines, make sure your children know that if they don't like a certain ingredient, they can usually be switched out. I mean, if you're making a 'chilli con carne', you can arguably switch the meat to make it 'chilli sans carne', you can adjust the amount of chilli you put in, but you probably can't remove the kidney beans because then it's no longer a chilli. But hey, just change the name and enjoy the meal you've made. I would much rather we had children who turn into adults that feel confident to create, than adults that need to rely on takeaways and expensive processed foods.

Art

So, with that being said, cooking and baking is an art. Presentation of food is definitely artistic. We mentioned creating patterns when decorating cakes or biscuits in the mathematical development section.

The autonomy to decorate, the freedom to create the way they want to do will show up in other areas. They can use different colours; you can buy sprinkles and decorations. It is a fun activity and I love to have some sort of decorating activity if there is a playdate as it tends to be a moment of calm, where they are all sat in one place, but also means they have social interactions and develop speaking and listening too.

With one child, we made an apple pie, and she made the most beautiful sculpture for the middle and used a fork to create a pattern around the outside.

If you do watch the cake tv programmes you will see that they make the most beautiful creations.

I have to premise this section with changes in how ideas have changed on how we use food for play. With parts of the world, and indeed in the current climate, children in First World Countries are also surviving on limited food, and so, we must be mindful of wasting food. Therefore, playing with food for playing's sake is more frowned upon than when I first became a teacher, or even when I was a child. If you are playing with food in your own home, there is no reason why it must ultimately be wasted, for example, when we were looking into colour and food dyes, we boiled the pasta to al dente, then separated into different bowls to experiment with different colours, seeing how much we needed to put in to create different colour pasta. We then used the rainbow concoction as part of our meal.

Rather than never using food in our experimentation or creation, I think we should just be more mindful about what we do next, which we will talk more about in the chapter on Sustainability.

Lots of these sections overlap; the above experiment is also science as well as creativity. Using penne pasta to make a necklace also helps our fine motor development as it is a threading activity. Using dough mixtures instead of playdough is fine motor but also sensory. Sensory exploration can also be enhanced by playing with different types of foods. Creativity and fine motor skills can be developed with potato or vegetable printing or making brushes by tying spaghetti together and only boiling the bottom half. A child that is not interested in picking up a pencil to mark make, might love the idea of using a spaghetti brush.

One tradition that overlaps history and culture as well as fine motor skills is the decorating or carving of pumpkins. Developmentally appropriate tasks can be differentiated here with the uptake of more people painting their pumpkins rather than carving them or handing your child a black pen to draw their designs on. When they do become better at cutting other snacks, then you can start to let them experiment with a carving kit. Just like in the section on health and safety, most accidents occur when you have implements that are too blunt for the job at hand, this being the time you are more likely to slip. The brilliant thing about pumpkin carving is the amount you can do with the pumpkin. Scooping out the seeds is a job most children can help with, it is a sensory experience and if you want to, you can dry the seeds to eat (or use them in another art project) but best of all is collecting the pumpkin, adding it with sweet potato and carrot for a delicious soup.

Actions

***decorate cakes or biscuits, show me on Instagram, tag @more_to_organising with the hashtags #moretomealtime #creativedevelopment**

***let me see your decorated pumpkins, tag @more_to_organising with the hashtags #moretomealtimes #pumpkindecorating**

Music

Using dried foods to create musical instruments has occurred throughout history. In African history, shakers were filled with seeds or kernels from maize. So just like I mentioned, many of these themes overlap. When learning about food, you can learn about instruments in history, and you can learn about African traditions. There is MORE TO everything. You just have to start thinking about everything in terms of, "What else can we learn from this?" I think the most wonderful thing about this journey is that you as an adult will learn so much too. There is something delicious about learning with the children. You are showing them that it is ok not to know something but also that every day we can learn something new. Speaking of things you can learn; this is new for me! I knew that people have made musical instruments from fruits and vegetables before but on checking the information, there is a whole orchestra from Austria that is touring this year (2023) where every instrument is made from dried fruits or vegetables. There are videos on YouTube and on their website, of them making and playing the instruments. This is where learning can cross over into technology, purposeful screen time to excite them to research further, to create something themselves, to learn more. I think the vegetable orchestra sounds amazing. If you do decide to make instruments with your food, please do research and be sensible, this is where those accidents can occur, don't let your children go wild with a carrot and a corkscrew and don't go wild yourself.

Luckily, you don't need to cut up any vegetables to make music in your kitchen. Using pans and wooden spoons for drums and sticks, shaking cutlery in a washing up bowl, or even the art of creating the sound on a wine glass (sans wine) by wetting your finger and circling around the rim. Once they have found they can do that, have a few wine glasses with different amounts of water in and listen to the different sounds.

When I was a classroom teacher, to warm up our vocal cords we exercised our mouths. One of the ways to help the children create different shapes with their mouths was to talk about 'sucky spaghetti' where you make your lips into a circle as though you're slurping spaghetti while making an 'oooooo' noise and an 'eeeeee' sound by widening the sides of your mouth to fit a watermelon. By switching between the two sounds, it warms up the muscles in your mouth ready for singing.

There are so many songs relating to food and drink. This links to communication and language, in listening and understanding but also helps children with rhyme, rhythm, alliteration and vocabulary.

The children and I often love to sing about the food we are eating, obviously, it is a choking hazard to speak or sing while eating so make sure it is while you're cooking or on breaks between bites.

Going back to changing the shape of our mouths, 'Apples and Bananas' is a lot of fun. The sentence is, "I like to eat, eat, eat apples and bananas." You start with pronouncing the fruit names as normal then you change to the long 'a' sound so it's more like 'ate ate ate', 'aypples' and 'baynaynays', then 'ee', 'eeples' and 'beeneenees' and you repeat it with 'igh' sound and so on.

Action Amanda's, 'Can you eat a rainbow?' song is brilliant for thinking about the colours on our plate like in the nutrition and planning sections of the book. There are so many nursery rhymes and children's songs related to food.

Actions

***find more songs with food in them**

***make an instrument with things in the kitchen, make a band with your family and record a food song, share on Instagram tagging @more_to_organising with the hashtags #moretomealtimes #kitchenband**

Chapter 5
Meal Planning

In my first full time nanny role, I created a 4-week meal plan, I had three children, and one was a toddler, so I also made sure lunch was different to create variety. In all the roles where there has not been a chef, I have been in charge of the menu planning, sourcing, and cooking. I think it is so important to provide balance and gut diversity.

I really feel passionate that the children should be involved in this aspect. As in the reading opportunities section, pouring over recipe books, going to the library to shake up your meal plans, changing your meal plans seasonally to make it more interesting and avoid getting into a boring rut but also, taking advantage of vegetables and fruit that are at their best in different seasons.

Meal planning stops you from getting to the fridge with hungry mouths and ending up feeding them pasta for the third time this week. It also means they are definitely getting a variety of different proteins and carbohydrates as well as vitamins. The best thing about planning is that it really can save you time and money.

I see Meal Planning as a kind of jigsaw, where you can't put the same pieces of the puzzle next to each other, as in pasta on Wednesday, Thursday, and Friday. Being a nanny, I generally work Monday to Friday. The weekend roles that I had, had chefs anyway so although I am going to work on the weekdays in this book, there is no reason why you can't make a plan for weekends too. The beauty of not planning every single meal means you can be a little more flexible, you can go to the grandparents for dinner, or to a restaurant for lunch or you can be spontaneous on those plan-free days. With meal planning, I do a lot of batch cooking and freezing, which means that if you do end up not following the plan, you don't waste the food and you can use it on another day. The way I set out my days means I always know what protein I am making that day.

Meat-Free Mondays

Try it (Chicken)Tuesdays!

Meat Wednesdays

Cheese Thursday

Fish Fridays

In the Tea sections, meal ideas that have been successful in many families will be suggested, but when you have a clearer idea what protein they will have each day, you then create two, three, or four-week menus, choosing different carbohydrates and vegetables.

I did a workshop for the Home Educators Conference and supported them with their meal planning. I did have a question which was, "Did they have to eat that on that particular day?" As explained in my second book, everything has to work for your particular family. In reality, when I make the meal plans, it is more of a guideline, it is ok to switch out the meals but I never have the thought, "Oh my goodness, what on earth will I make for tea tonight?" as I have lots of ideas to hand, and as I said above, within the plan, I batch cook and freeze, so for many days out of the month, I am just pulling it out of the freezer to defrost and adding to it to make it a balanced meal.

When I was working with school aged children and a toddler, many times I would make sure there was a couple of portions for our lunch the next day if we were not out at a class or visiting a museum.

Actions

***head to www.moretoorganising.com to print your meal planning format- share your plans on Instagram tagging @more_to_organising with the hashtags #moretomealtimes #mealplan**

Chapter 6
Meal Ideas

Breakfast

I am of the generation that was brought up on sugary cereals. It was so bad that I even used to put sugar on Ricicles and Frosties. I don't really know how I got away with that. Even in Juniors, I would eat Rusks for breakfast and when I got to Secondary school, as soon as I got in from school, I would have about three bowls of cereal while watching CBBC.

The morning routine seems to be the most stressful for my clients. Many parents have told me about the rush, the stress, the problems of getting the kids fed and out the door on time. I currently have twins in the morning. I arrive at 07:07 am, and, as the children wave their mum off at the window, I start on breakfast. They are allowed to watch their iPads until breakfast is made. I always make sure I sit down with them while they eat. We have brilliant chats in this time. While I am washing up, they set up a game for us to play. I set everything up by the door; their bags (checking they have their snack, water bottle and reading books) and their bikes. We then have 20 minutes to play. At 5 minutes to 8, I tell them we have five minutes left. At two minutes to 8, we all have one last turn and then we have a "race" to the bathroom (children against adults), and we do their teeth and sun cream as it is summer at the moment. We then get to continue the game after teeth time. At about quarter past, we get our shoes on, and we are out the door. It is as calm as it all sounds. In Winter, we used to get ready at ten past 8, just to give us time to get our hats, scarves, gloves, and raincoats on. Because the children know the routine, it is easy. Having a breakfast routine is as important as the breakfast meal itself and I will share some menu suggestions with you in a moment.

In my second book, I wrote about another school run experience when I was a wrap-around Nanny in Kew. The children were addicted to their iPad from 7am and wanted them all evening too. You noticed; the twins had their iPad for 5 minutes with me. I am not against screen time. Even as adults, we spend a lot of time on screens. As with supporting their development with food, we also need to help our children have balance with screen time. With the wraparound children (and working as a team with the parents) iPad-filled mornings turned into games of monopoly, and the afternoons turned into baking and craft.

I also had an ad hoc client where I just took the toddler to nursery. She usually wasn't hungry as soon as she woke up, so I would prepare her breakfast, offer it to her at home but if she didn't finish it, it wasn't a problem. She would eat fruit and a croissant on the way sitting in the pram. In all honesty, I also find it hard to eat as soon as I wake up. I had to readjust my own morning routine when my start time went from 7.30 to 7.15 but also, the weather made an impact too. When I didn't have to arrive until half past, I ate breakfast before work. I am an early riser and I love to pop my washing machine on, so it runs while I do the school run, which I call habit overlapping. I like to do my social media posts for my business in that sweet hour where I am not receiving emails or have any meetings. But just that fifteen-minute difference meant I had to rethink the whole routine. I just can't face breakfast that early so I would have porridge as soon as I got in from doing the school run. As the weather got warmer, hot porridge was the last thing I wanted. I did dabble with overnight oats, which I do love. Since having the diagnosis of low good cholesterol, I am making more of an effort to add salmon and avocado into my breakfast routine, adding them to toast or scrambled eggs. The reason I am telling you this is because we need to shake up our routines every now and then. We get into ruts or in my case, external factors will impact our day, so we have to re-optimise our routines. What worked before may no longer serve you.

Being a nanny means it is literally my job to get the children dressed, fed, packed and out the door, and I appreciate that parents have other things to think about. That is why I work with parents to optimise their routines and space, so then at least the mornings can run a bit more smoothly. One trick I do so there is less washing up and I have made sure they have their water bottles for the day, is to serve drinks in their water bottles during breakfast. That way, when I clear the table, I just pop them in their book bags. They have very rarely drunk so much to warrant me needing to refill them again.

Megan Rossi, author of 'Eat Well, Live More,' talks about following science and adjusting habits slightly. She talks about adding vegetables into breakfast. So below is how to do that citing some instances that have worked for children I have cared for.

Poo Juice-Avo- I looked after a child who ended up with constipation as she didn't eat a balanced diet. The main thing I took away from this was that she learnt that if she didn't eat, then she would be offered other options that were not necessarily good for her body and digestion. It wasn't that she didn't eat different types of foods. I did see that there was a big fuss made when she didn't eat, mealtimes were a huge deal, she got a lot of attention. Now, this child was a toddler, so she was not doing anything consciously and attention seeking behaviours are absolutely valid. I know it is hard when you are emotionally attached, i.e., a parent, and of course, as a nanny, I am emotionally attached to the children too, just not as much, I don't have that unbreakable bond, but believe me when I say that I love all the children I have cared for from the bottom of my heart. And with this child, (I was overnight too, so I was there in the depth of the night) I would say, I probably fell for her deeper than any other child partly due to the fact that I was there for her throughout the night also.

If a child is offered a balance of foods, and they choose to eat what they eat, there should be no forcing of food or even any comment in front of them. This child ended up with awful constipation which needed medicine to help digestion. There are so many emotions involved when our children are not eating. It is a tricky slope as we don't want to end up with children who end up with eating disorders, like the two I mentioned when I was a teacher at the beginning of the book. I always talk about decluttering our language as well as our space. So, we ended up making this delicious poo juice with avocado, spinach, prunes, cacao, honey, and milk, and she lapped it up. It was sweet and chocolatey.

Smoothie Bowls- creating our own smoothies is a lot of fun, having a thick smoothie in a bowl means you can add vegetables in the liquid section but create a pretty picture with fruits sliced up. You can even add chocolate drops on the top for a lovely morning treat. If they are dark chocolate nibs, even better.

Overnight oats- the ultimate time saving food. With one family, the child and I made a few jars of overnight oats, packed with dried fruits- apricots, raisins, sultanas, and cranberries to name a few - and although I don't eat nuts, we also crushed nuts to add in. Add a plant-based milk with some honey all mixed up. It can be saved for up to 4-5 days so just spoon your portion out daily. To add a vegetable in there, grate a carrot or even a courgette for extra nutrients.

Savoury Scones- I started looking after a child whose teeth were not healthy. She had to have a baby tooth taken out and replaced with a metal tooth, so the gap didn't close before her adult tooth came through. So, I started looking into all the different things we could have for breakfast that reduced the sugar intake. While brushing our teeth is the habit we need to get into, another habit we can get into is eating less foods that cause such problems too. With the involvement of the child, we looked over lots of recipes that she might like to try, so savoury scones and some warm breakfasts discussed below were the solution. Now I know what you're going to say! "But Kathryn, we don't have enough time in the morning!" I hear you. It is just about getting into routine, batch cooking, freezing, and having a plan. I am not expecting you to whip up some scones before school, but you can make them together the night before or even the weekend before. The brilliant thing is that they do freeze, so just pull a couple out the night before. We made ours with chives and then I fried some bacon bits or pancetta while she was getting dressed. I didn't have just one child, there was also a teenager. There was also a Stay at Home Mum, and a baby that we sometimes made things for too.

Warm breakfasts

I am not reinventing the wheel here, I am just showing you options that are not toast or cereal, which also can mean you add vegetables in.

Egg Muffins - now, I did make these in the morning, but I don't think it takes very long. Whisk up some eggs, add in grated cheese, chopped up tomatoes or get creative and add in cut up peppers or mushrooms (I don't like them, but you do you). You just pop them in bun cases and put them in the oven for about 10 minutes. We liked to add pancetta again, like the savoury scones. The good news is that they last in the fridge for 5 days in a Tupperware box, so you can batch cook them and eat them all week long.

Porridge- Like the overnight oats, you can add in grated vegetables quite easily. With a little grated carrot, you can make a pseudo carrot cake concoction. I do always make this in the morning, but you can prep the carrot the night before and add in honey for sweetness.

Blueberry pancake bites- These can be batch cooked and frozen too! Make a pancake mixture, pop in some blueberries, and put in bun cases. They only take about 12 minutes in the oven. Okay, this one doesn't have a vegetable, but it's about balance.

Dinner

So, I have said it before and I will say it again, school dinner and Christmas dinner happen at the meal in the middle of the day. Dinner ladies in schools, work at the meal in the middle of the day. So, all those people saying dinner is the evening meal are...also correct. I think that dinner is a hot meal. In the evening, I think dinner is like a fancy meal, so what I make for the children in the evening, I wouldn't call that a dinner. So, this section is for the weekends or the school holidays when they are not on a trip to a museum, where I would take a packed lunch, and not the meal I would give them in the afternoon, as I am northern and that is called tea. Not to be confused with a cup of tea. When I first moved to London, one family called that meal 'supper' which to me is the snack you have before you go to bed. Being a linguist, I just joke about these idiosyncrasies as I believe variation in accents and words are good.

I think the key to this meal is making your life easier. Being mindful of what they had for breakfast and what they will have for tea to provide gut variety.

When I was a little girl, I used to go to church with my childhood best friend, and we would always beg to have a playdate. While we were not successful every time, whenever I did go to her house, we always had cheese on toast. It was quick and easy, we all wolfed it down happily and although I can't remember whether it was served with any vegetables, we definitely had yogurt and fruit.

Whenever I didn't go to her house, it was usually because we went to my grandparents for a roast dinner. So, whenever we got home on a Sunday evening, we always had dippy egg (or soft-boiled egg with soldiers) while watching Last of the Summer Wine and Blind Date. This is like a core memory. We rarely got to eat in front of the television, so this was super special. While clearly dippy egg could be for tea as well as lunch, it is obviously great as a breakfast too. I love how versatile eggs are; how many different things you can make with them and how you can eat it for everything and even as a snack. As in the nutrition section, it is a great form of protein, and it lends itself to serving vegetables with it too. I have dipped asparagus in dippy egg as well as soldiers- which are great to discuss science with our children and ask them how long it takes to move through your body.

Dinner can be leftovers from the night before, or rather, when you plan to eat the same things the day after, you plan for it and make more on purpose, pop it in a container before serving so you definitely have a portion. This doesn't always work if you are going on a trip the next day to a museum or a park but can work if you have a thermal to take it with you, see packed lunch for more info.

If you are not having yesterday's meal, I really think it is important to make your life easy. While the children are at school and you have a toddler at home, adding lettuce, if it lends itself to it, to your own meal and eating the same as them saves time and money. Quiche, omelette, beans on toast, cheese on toast, soup, sandwich, wraps, served with different vegetables and fruit. We don't want to eat bread all day every day, but with the different breakfast options as seen in that section, it frees up space for a bread option later in the day. And remember, most of the time, you will both be eating what you ate the evening before, so these are not everyday options. Balance is key.

Action

***plan to make extra so you can eat it for lunch, take a photo and tag @more_to_organising on Instagram with the #moretomealtimes #savetimesavemoney #leftoverlunch**

Packed Lunch

Queen of batch cooking, I also used what we made the night before for the teenager's lunch. Having a thermal pot, as soon as I arrived at work, I would add boiling water into the thermal at the same time I made cups of tea, I would pop the meal in the microwave and then go up to wake the children up. When we came back down, I would drain the pot and add in the hot food ready for the packed lunch, adding in a fork if it was pasta and a spoon if it was soup. Whether she had a sandwich or hot meal, I would still add a vegetable and fruit. Every now and again, I would get her chocolate edamame beans as a little treat.

With this family, we switched from Mum's house to Dad's house every Friday, so just making sure we didn't accidentally take spoons on the last day made life easier. The sucky yogurts mean no spoons need to be taken to school at all.

As the teenager was older, it was her responsibility to bring the flask or lunchbox down and empty it at dinner time, so it could be repacked the next day. If she wasn't having a warm meal, which I prepped, the idea was that she made her own, and while she did, during exam stress, I just took that burden from her; I wanted to make sure she was getting the right brain food rather than rushing at the last minute and being hungry when she had other things to concentrate on.

I lined the smoothies, suckies and fruit up in the fridge with enough for the week and one extra for Monday, so packing was even easier and all that was to be made was the salmon and cream cheese bagel in the morning. Sometimes, if I had roasted a chicken, she would have chicken sandwiches instead. I then add a chopped-up vegetable too; carrot, cucumbers, peppers, tomatoes… (although that's a fruit!).

If you can get into the habit of making as much the night before, creating systems to make life easier, and get into a good routine, things like packed lunches will rarely become annoying again.

Action

***set up your fridge with a packed lunch station, post a picture on Instagram tagging @more_to_organising with the hashtags #moretomealtimes #savetime**

Tea

As in the chapter on Meal Planning, I will talk about anecdotes of successful meal ideas in the categories. These are not all the ideas, sometimes it is as simple as a jigsaw, piecing together a protein, carbohydrate, and vegetables, switching it up from the day before, ensuring you have pasta, rice, potato, couscous, or other carbohydrate not back-to-back and indeed, not for lunch and tea. Please remember this is a guideline, it is not set, and it is just to make life easier. Having a library of ideas means you can pick and choose more easily; it takes the stress away. If your children do not like a meal, then take it out of rotation. This is what has worked for some of the families I have cooked for.

<u>Monday - Meat- free</u>

Pesto Pasta has to be the main go-to meat-free meal for all the families I have worked for, that, and tomato and mascarpone pasta. I have been very lucky in that many children I have looked after have loved omelettes. A jacket potato with beans or cheese is also good, although this one can also be on Cheese Thursdays.

<u>Tuesday - Try it with chicken</u>

We couldn't have got more 'try it' than our experimentation with spaghetti carbonara, which we often added chicken into as well. I supported an 8-year-old to perfect this meal to her liking, by finding as many recipes as we could and trying every single one. The teenage sister would rate her concoctions too. If you are having pasta on Monday, you wouldn't want spaghetti on Tuesday, so trying a new chicken curry with rice, or making your own home-made chicken nuggets with mash are other options. I have spoken about our mash-people, which makes my children ask for mash, but it can easily be sweet potato instead. I personally love sweet potato and I have had some children who have also loved it.

A roast chicken dinner with all the trimmings always went down really well.

Whatever you do have, add something that they have never tried before, this could be a different way to make something, or a new vegetable they have researched when they made the rainbow, even a different type of fruit. Here, we are trying to get them into the habit of trying something different. It is ok not to like something. Congratulate them for giving it a go.

<u>Wednesday - Meat</u>

One of the most successful dishes was a rainbow sausage dish, where tinned tomato, cubes of carrot, sweetcorn, peas, and red onion, (are they red or purple?) were cooked and added to a casserole dish with sausages... which went down even better when we swapped tinned tomatoes with beans! From my years of feeding children, I honestly feel like it is a win if they are willingly eating 5 vegetables in one meal alone. Adding garlic and herbs to taste, this dish can be served with literally any carb.

Bolognese is without a doubt the most versatile base, I love it so much as you can easily batch cook as much as you wish, if you start with the onions, meat, and tinned tomatoes you can separate one half into another pan, adding different herbs or spices, creating one into a Bolognese and the other into a chilli with kidney beans and chilli. You obviously don't make it over spicy.

Another really successful meal was a stew and dumplings.

I have found that some children do not like meals where everything is mixed together, and in that case, some of these meals don't lend themselves to that. The rainbow sausage casserole could easily be served separately.

<u>Thursday - Cheese</u>

As mentioned, jacket potato with cheese, if you didn't have it on Monday, is a good option here but I love cheese so much. I like to have halloumi with green quinoa, where you blend quinoa with cooked broccoli and peas (something I learnt from Nutritionist, Maddy Karlsson) and squeezed with lemon; while that might be a recipe you think your children wouldn't like, until they try it, you will never know.

My children love cheese toasties or cheese melted in tortilla wraps in a frying pan. This is not something I give often and if you have had a sandwich or wrap for lunch, then you wouldn't have it again in the evening, but as we have said a million times, it is about balance and making your life easier.

While omelette can also be served on Monday, if you didn't have that then or for lunch, you could have a cheesy omelette today.

<u>Friday - Fish</u>

In one family I worked for, the children loved prawn noodle soup. This is a brilliant dish as the traditional way is to add the vegetables into the soup alongside the noodles and the prawns, with prawn stock. If your children don't like the same vegetables, you can create a 'make your own' station, where they get to add in what they love, or even, keep them on their side plate and eat them alongside. The point here is that the aim is to get them eating their vegetables, and if this strategy empowers them enough, then we are on to a winner.

Salmon in teriyaki sauce is also loved, alongside noodles or rice, we always enjoyed it with edamame beans. Some things just go easily together.

Fishcakes, while making a messy blender, also always seem popular. These usually have a potato or sweet potato base, so there is no need to add extra carbohydrates. Just up the vegetables.

While as a family, you will obviously still need to feed those little mouths at the weekend, I usually find its good to have some open spaces in your plan, so while you have planned for 5 meals every week, inevitably, there might be a playdate or a meal at a relative's house, you might choose to go to a restaurant or have a takeaway. It is all about balance, so instead of overplanning and getting stuck on the plan, having free days where you just cook what you feel like every now and again, makes it even less rigid. I will also say, sometimes we would switch up the days, depending on if we needed a quick meal due to an unforeseen event. That way, you can just move the meal you were going to have that day to the weekend.

While some people might get het up on the logistics of the whole thing, I have found that children feel more comfortable and even excited for mealtimes when they have been involved and know what they are having. In the appendix, is a table you can use to create your own meal plans. I have spoken about 15 different meals that my little ones over the last 9 years have loved, but there are so many more meals. Head to www.moretoorganising.com for more ideas.

Actions

***share your meat free Monday and Try it Tuesday meals on Instagram, tagging @more_to_organising with the hashtags #moretomealtimes #meatfreemonday #tryittuesday**

Chapter 7

Snack ideas

One of the strangest snacks that was never available when I was a child is seaweed, along with the chocolate edamame beans from Itsu, but also available in Tesco. The thing with these snacks is that they are still processed, however; we talked about balance. If you eat one hundred of anything, you will feel sick. There is some nutritional value and having seaweed or edamame beans as an option every now and again will be fine. I had never actually had edamame beans until I moved to London, but I love them, covered in chocolate or otherwise.

I think the thing about snacks is that they usually have to be transportable, easy to eat on the go. The reason why processed snacks are so popular is because they are easy to grab, packaged individually and are usually portioned.

With the wraparound job, I would get to the family house before pick-up to do any prep I needed to do, but also bring a snack. They had quite a long scoot home in terms of school runs or we had to go to ballet or another sports club, so I took three snacks each. A vegetable, a fruit and 'other' which was a small portion of something processed like bread sticks. Just providing vegetables and fruit doesn't fill up their tummies as much and inevitably, they will have a sugar crash, so having all three options to have in - whichever order they wished - not only made them feel like they had autonomy, but also gave them the fuel and nutrients they needed to get us dancing, sporting and all the way home.

Summer Snacks

Not that you can't use some of these during the colder months, but there are certain snacks that provide a refreshing, cooling sensation. There was one time that I put the fire on in Winter so I could have ice cream, but that's a whole other story. As we spoke in the chapter on Nutrition, it's about balance, so ice creams and ice pops have a time and a place, but also providing scrumptious snacks with diverse nutritional value is a win-win.

Frozen Bananas

I once did an Insta Reel on freezing my bananas which got a lot of views and lots of likes. (I did have another reel get 31,000 views!!) Go and check them out by following me on Instagram @more_to_organising. It is such a simple idea that I first discovered while working as a nanny in Italy during the summers. Peel the bananas, wrap them in cling film (or reusable wrap) and pop them in the freezer for 1-2 hours. My bananas tend to go brown before I get to them all, so when they are on the turn, that's when I usually decide to put them in the freezer. It extends their shelf-life, so they don't go to waste.

If you have more time, mashing the bananas with a fork in a Tupperware box creates a banana ice cream. I personally don't think it needs sweetening, but you can put a teaspoon of honey or maple syrup in. I did a nutrition course for my own health and learnt that you have to be careful which maple syrups you buy as some can be maple syrup sauces which means they are processed and have things added to them.

Yogurt Bark

This is another thing we used to make a lot in Italy. Using Greek yogurt, add a little honey or maple syrup for sweetness, and on a baking tray lined with baking paper, pour on the yogurt to make a slab. On the slab, you place sliced strawberries, halved blueberries, pretty much any fruit on top, and the bit the children love the best is grated dark chocolate. You can use dairy milk too as the amount you put on is minimal. Our favourite thing was to add strawberry yogurt to the Greek yogurt which enhances the flavour, but the children also loved to swirl the two colours. You can switch it up. The best thing about making yogurt bark is you can be as experimental as you like. Use blueberry yogurt as your colour and make patterns with your toppings. The thinner your bark, the quicker it will be to freeze but allow at least three hours. When it comes out, an adult can score it with a knife, snapping it into triangles and using a paper towel so it is not too cold on little hands.

Fruit and Veg

I know fruit as a snack is obvious, but I don't know about you, I love watermelon as a cooling snack. It is really good for their water intake. Or even a good melon boat. While I do offer fruit all year round, cutting an orange into segments for the children to suck the juice out seems to be welcome on a hot sunny day.

Simply freezing your fruit is a great way to have a cold snack. You can buy bags of summer berries, blueberries, raspberries or even pineapple. Pulling them out five minutes before eating them or running them under cold water can help to soften them.

Again, raw vegetables are brilliant all year round, then providing snacks to help cool our children down just means we can change how we provide them. I know many children who love frozen peas, it gives a sensory experience as well as a cooling effect.

Frozen sweetcorn is also an option, but it must be noted that there is a rare infection from the bacteria called Listeria which can cause diarrhoea and sickness. This can be very dangerous for babies, so this is not an option for them (or our grandparents)

Ice Pops

If you're going to freeze juice, putting a teaspoon of icing sugar makes sure it is sweet enough to enjoy after it has frozen. With one child, she was especially excited to make home-made traffic light ice pops. We made the colours by juicing the fruits and we added different juices for the base. Making sure the first segment was fully frozen before adding the next could be added, taught her the importance of being patient. As in the next chapter, we are going to talk about habits and rewards, making ice pops is about getting into a habitual practice so you always have them available. It is hard to batch create these as in all the families I have worked in, there are only so many moulds you can have but also, the freezer space doesn't allow for this. The great thing about making a new batch every few days is that you can adjust your recipe, switch up the flavours and just have fun with your creations. These can take up to 6 hours to freeze so always plan to make them at least the day before. Apparently, they last up to 12 months in the freezer, I don't know about your family, but the ice pops we have made have always been gobbled up within a week of making them!

Winter Snacks

Cheese twists

Making puff pastry from scratch is a great task to do with your children when you have got a lot of time on your hands, but an alternative is to buy pre-made puff pastry which can make the process quicker and fun.

When I was doing Food Technology in Year 9, we had to make pastries. You know the plastic container you get when you buy two slices of cheesecake? Well, I decided to make a savoury pasty and a sweet pasty, and package them together so people could have a main and a dessert on the go. I thought I was a genius. Why not experiment with what you can create?

Snacks in winter just need to be not as cooling! There are many times we come back from a dark, cold, rainy school run, change them into snuggly pjs and have a hot chocolate to warm them up. Warm milk or hot chocolate has high protein content so can be a snack, although it contains tryptophan which helps with sleep. Timing this snack might be helpful before bedtime.

Actions

***show us your home-made snacks on Instagram tagging @more_to_organising with the hashtags #moretomealtimes #homemadesnacks**

Chapter 8

Habits and Rewards

Food should never be used as a reward.

When children are growing, they need more food. There are a lot of children's nutritionists that say not to comment on how much children are eating. When you say something to a child, no matter how flippant, they may take it on and form habits as a result. When the children I work with ask for seconds or thirds, the only comment I will say is, "Wow, your body is growing," or talk about all the hard work they did at swimming or football or gymnastics that has meant their body needs fuel.

We also form habits with foods related to how we are feeling. When your children are asking for snacks, encourage them to think about why they might want one. For example, we reach in the cupboard when we are bored, tired, sad, and even thirsty. If we are not in tune with our bodies, sometimes we mistake thirst for being hungry. If possible, always have a glass of water to check that we are not thirsty. When I bring the children in from school, they are starving! You would think that they hadn't eaten all day. Interestingly, they had a double playdate today and not one of them asked for a snack because they were too excited to get on with playing. I did mention this in the snack section, but providing a raw snack, laid out on the plates ready for tea, means they can eat them while they are waiting for the rest of the meal to cook.

We can adjust our habits, but it is easier to form healthy ones in the first place. Habits such as creating meal plans, batch cooking, eating a rainbow and storing foods to make life easier will be something that they take into adulthood. Have a think about something that you always do because that's how you were taught when you were a child. I have an example. When I was a teenager, I somehow picked up the habit of tapping on the top of a drinks can, purportedly to do something to the bubbles to stop the liquid from over-frothing when I opened it. Now, I cannot not tap the top. I can say that they never overflow, but whether they would have in the first place, I will never know. Having fizzy drinks is ok every now and again, but don't get in the habit of drinking them every day like I did at university.

My mum told me a story of a girl that always cut the ends off the beef joint and one day, when someone asked her why, she said that it was the way she was told to do it when she was younger. It turned out that they had a thinner oven, apparently, slimline ovens are 10cms thinner than the average oven. So sometimes, we do things because we were taught, and we just continue these habits without questioning them. It is a bit like me putting salt in the pasta/potato/vegetable water, although that did turn out to be for flavour and mildly scientific too. I have been asked to make things that I have never cooked before, and while I can figure out how to cook things, I prefer to ask the parents how they do it as the children are more likely to eat the meal if it is made in a similar way.

One thing I do know from cooking in several different households is that common sense is not common, and I am not saying that means there is only one way to do things, I just mean, there are actually different ways to do the same thing. Sometimes when we support children to learn, especially in maths, it is great to show them different ways to do the same thing so they can find the way that they feel works for them best. Obviously, there are some things that have to be done a certain way such as safe ways to cut things or making sure meat is thoroughly cooked through.

What we want to do is help our children to have the will to learn how to make different things, even if they haven't come across them in the past. The best way to do this is to get in the habit of trying to cook new recipes and doing different techniques, in a developmentally appropriate way. Getting the children to see you try new things also helps them to know that it is ok not to know how to do everything and that we are always able to learn.

Stop using food as rewards! This can lead to unhealthy relationships with food. At one end, it might create a link to comfort which is a hard habit to get out of and on the other end, it can lead to serious eating disorders. Instead, look for other things to reward our children. As a Professional Family Organiser, I don't even suggest you reward with physical items either. What is left? Verbal rewards are amazing for self-esteem. Experiences or spending time together are so valuable. These don't have to cost a lot. Also, if you do have more than one child, sometimes, giving one child special one-to-one quality time is a great reward. It could be baking together. It could be doing a food science experiment. Showing love by buying children things is not what your children will remember. Showing love through spending time with them will bring connection and memories. If you still want to have something physical, young children love a stamp. It's brilliant because it washes off! Stickers for our young children are the bees' knees! As a teacher, I did have a box with useful things as rewards. They had to do something amazing to get something from there. Think smelly pencils, rubbers, gel pens, highlighters etc These are fun, don't take up much space and can be used for something purposeful, like writing the recipes or shopping lists.

Actions

*** create a new healthy habit for your family**

*** show us your new reward ideas and tag @more_to_organising with the hashtags #moretomealtimes #foodisnotareward**

Chapter 9
Sustainability

Helping children to get in the habit of eating food with balance is for their future. Sustainability is also for their future. There are lots of things helping us return to reusing items and thinking about nature. On the walk home, I always say thank you when the children give me their litter from their snack. The main reason I do this is, so the litter doesn't get dropped into the environment by accident. I had a conversation with the five-year-old recently and she said, I wish snacks didn't have wrappers. So, we talked about bananas and oranges having biodegradable 'wrappers' but also, that we could buy snacks in bulk and decant them into Tupperware, meaning we could wash and reuse them and there would be less packaging. In other roles, as I have mentioned, this is what we did. For my personal snacking, I found these cute reusable zip lock bags instead of using plastic bags, and the nanny family have started to use paper bags for sandwiches which is slightly better for the environment. There are also beeswax covers that can be used to keep our foods fresh, and silicone covers to top open containers. The thing about all of this is that they are habits that you have to commit to. It will be harder for us to change our habits than to form good habits from the get-go. I remember getting milk bottles as a child at my own house and my grandma's. My grandma hated the milk bottle being placed on the table so we would put it on and count to see how long it would take her to notice. My mum also used to do that when she was a child. Sometimes you'd have to scrape tiny slugs off the bottle so I guess I can see where she is coming from. But then you'd put the bottle out on the doorstep and the milkman would switch it.

There is an uprise of dried food shops where you take your own containers and pay for just the weight of what you decant. If that is too much, start by buying huge and decanting into smaller sections. This means the packaging is less. If we do have packaging, making something useful with them can be the most beneficial for the earth. Or just make something fun with the packaging and then recycle it. Junk Modelling is great for their creative development, it helps with their decision making and problem-solving skills and most of all, it is fun.

The best way to support the environment is to reduce our meat consumption. I am not vegetarian, although I was one briefly at university. While I do care about the animals, I actually did it to become more adventurous with foods. When I went to restaurants, I always had the same meals, and it really worked. After my short stint, I developed a wider variety of meals that I would enjoy and cook. And while I did dabble in the miniscule options back then of meat alternatives, I quickly realised that I didn't want to replace meat with processed, man-made options. I now make sure I have vegetarian or even vegan days at least twice a week, although that is not to say I eat meat for every meal even on the other days.

The next thing we can do to be more sustainable is to eat food grown locally as much as possible. Mainly with that I mean, eat food that hasn't had to travel very far. If you can't do that, make sure the food you are eating has been grown sustainably. Switch to companies that have sustainability at the heart of their ethos.

The other thing we can do is minimise food waste. With a few families, I placed the food in the middle of the table and the children could serve themselves. This has many benefits as it means the children have autonomy over what is on their plate, the amount that is on their plate and to listen to their body for when they are full but also, it means whatever is left in the middle of the table is easily packed away in the fridge. I would usually plan to eat the leftovers for my own lunch. My grandma taught me how to use the whole carcass after a roast chicken dinner as I mentioned in the ideas for Tea.

Actions

***switch individual packed snacks to large bags and decant into Tupperware**

***switch to reusable options (bees wax wrappers, reusable silicon lids etc) show me on Instagram tagging @more_to_organising with the hashtags #moretomealtimes #sustainable**

***swap at least two meals to meat free**

***eat seasonably and locally as much as possible**

Useful Websites or articles

Eatseasonably.co.uk

Twinkl.com

www.gov.uk/food-safety-your-responsibilities

WWW.CONTEMPORARY-AFRICAN-ART.COM

Vegetableorchestra.org

Reclaiming Mealtimes and child health and wellbeing by Fiese Bh (2008)

"I know why its yum, Mum" www.natashagavin,com

Cookbooks Kat Loves

Ella's Kitchen- Easy Family Cookbook

Feeding kids- The netmums.com cookery book

Annabel Karmel- Real Food Kids will love

Annebel Karmel's Fun, Fast and Easy Childrens Cookbook

Work with me…

I can't wait to see all the wonderful activities, recipes and new habits you form from reading this book. I hope you and your children have learnt and had fun in the kitchen and that mealtimes are so much happier and easier.

If your kitchen is still causing you hassle, I do in-person organisation services to support you to declutter, systemise and make your lives even easier and not just your kitchen. If there are any routines that are causing chaos in your family life, decluttering and organising can help.

If you live further afield, I have online support. Alternatively, buy, 'More to Organising- how to help your child become more independent and make your life easier' or if you want to bring more learning to life in the home, get yourself a copy of, 'There's More to Books than Reading- how to help your child bring stories to life.'

I also do workshops for nurseries, events, and parent groups.

With thanks to…

I want to thank my grandma for showing me the life skills I needed to cook from scratch (and the Teletubbies for showing me how to make egg mayonnaise). She lives on through the recipes she taught me.

I'd like to thank my Mum and Dad for supporting me and for working so hard when my brother and I were teenagers, which meant we argued over who got to cook so we didn't have to eat each other's food- he made everything with beans- I like beans but not every day- it's about (you guessed it) balance!

A special thanks goes to Action Amanda for being so supportive, for helping me with a wonderful book launch and for writing the foreword for this book.

With thanks to all my wonderful nanny children who feature heavily in all my books and my heart and to their parents for letting me be part of their precious children's lives. It is an honour to support them grow.

To my wonderful friend, Jenny that has to endure my long phone calls of all my crazy ideas.

I also want to thank UK Nanny, The Clean and Tidy Home Show and The Childcare and Education Expo for my speaking opportunities, networking and support as I have grown.

And last of all, thank you to you, the readers.

Love Kat x

Testimonials

Kathryn is an exceptional professional who truly loves working with children. Kathryn is confident in her approach and her calm and caring nature ensures that the children's best interests are at the heart of all her decisions. I have worked in the field of Education for over 25 years and Kathryn is a wonderful member of our profession.

I know she will continue to make a difference in children's lives as she has done with my own!

Liz, Acton

Within a couple of hours, Kat harmonised our kitchen. She showed us all the things we hadn't used in months (and often were buying over and over again) and organised out cupboards in a way that we can always see what we've got and can use up without shopping. In the run up to Christmas she's absolutely saved us money- so many of the ingredients we found in our badly organised cupboards, I would have gone out and bought for baking. She's cleared out our surfaces and left us with a kitchen we can enjoy cooking in. Plus, now we can see everything it's much easier to plan our shopping and avoid falling back into the same bad habits.

Jo, London

Kathryn has done an amazing job in helping me organise my home. She worked with us for one month and took her time for each room to come up with a clear and logical system. I can only recommend her service.

Everything is more in order and there is a logical system behind it. Especially helpful was the rotating system for my daughter's toys.

Charlotte, Kensal Rise

I LOVED being in my kitchen this week, It's less stressful. I still have a few cupboards to go but overall, it's been so amazing. I love my kitchen again. I can USE my kitchen again!

Courtney, Salem, USA (online client)

Follow me on Instagram

@more_to_organising

@more_to_mealtimes

@more_to_education

Email me on moretoorganising@gmail.com

Printed in Great Britain
by Amazon

27928631R00079